*Thomas Love Peacock*

THE PROFILES IN LITERATURE SERIES

GENERAL EDITOR: B. C. SOUTHAM, M.A., B.LITT. (OXON.)
*Formerly Department of English, Westfield College, University of London*

*Volumes in the series include*

| | |
|---|---|
| CHARLOTTE BRONTË | Arthur Pollard *University of Hull* |
| CHARLES DICKENS | Martin Fido, *University of Leeds* |
| HENRY FIELDING | C. J. Rawson, *University of Warwick* |
| JAMES JOYCE | Arnold Goldman, *University of Sussex* |
| HERMAN MELVILLE | D. E. S. Maxwell, *Professor of English, York Univ. Toronto* |
| SAMUEL RICHARDSON | A. M. Kearney, *Chorley College of Education* |
| WALTER SCOTT | Robin Mayhead, *University of Ghana* |
| JONATHAN SWIFT | Kathleen Williams, *University of California* |
| ZOLA | Philip Walker, *University of California* |

# *Thomas Love Peacock*

*by Carl Dawson*
*Department of English*
*University of California*
*Berkeley*

LONDON
**ROUTLEDGE & KEGAN PAUL**
NEW YORK: HUMANITIES PRESS

*First published 1968*
*by Routledge and Kegan Paul Ltd*
*Broadway House, 68–74 Carter Lane*
*London, E.C.4*

*Printed in Great Britain*
*by Northumberland Press Limited*
*Gateshead*



SBN 7100 2947 0

## *The Profiles in Literature Series*

This series is designed to provide the student of literature and the general reader with a brief and helpful introduction to the major novelists and prose writers in English, American and foreign literature.

Each volume will provide an account of an individual author's writing career and works, through a series of carefully chosen extracts illustrating the major aspects of the author's art. These extracts are accompanied by commentary and analysis, drawing attention to particular features of the style and treatment. There is no pretence, of course, that a study of extracts can give a sense of the works as a whole, but this selective approach enables the reader to focus his attention upon specific features, and to be informed in his approach by experienced critics and scholars who are contributing to the series.

The volumes will provide a particularly helpful and practical form of introduction to writers whose works are extensive or which present special problems for the modern reader, who can then proceed with a sense of his bearings and an informed eye for the writer's art.

An important feature of these books is the extensive reference list of the author's works and the descriptive list of the most useful biographies, commentaries and critical studies.

B.C.S.

# Contents

# *Thomas Love Peacock—his life and works*

## *Introduction*

Thomas Love Peacock is one of few writers of his generation remembered for his comedy. He stands apart, like Byron and Jane Austen, from an age that had more than its share of literary earnestness. Although in some of his writings he could be both sober and sentimental, Peacock was usually ironic. He shared none of the optimism of men like Macaulay, none of the zeal of men like Carlyle. In years of great social, political, and literary upheavals, Peacock remained a skeptical and laughing critic who judged his times on the basis of what he thought to be better times—whether Periclean Athens or eighteenth-century England—and who wrote with the independence and detachment of an outsider.

If Peacock is remembered for his comic novels, for *Headlong Hall, Nightmare Abbey*, and *Crotchet Castle*, he was nevertheless much more than a novelist. In fact his seven novels occupied only about two or three of his more than eighty years. He was also a translator and a scholar, an essayist and a poet. He composed verses before Wordsworth and Coleridge issued *Lyrical Ballads*, in 1798, and he published essays as late as the 1860's, when Matthew

Arnold published *Essays in Criticism* and T. H. Huxley *Man's Place in Nature.* He was a man of wide interests who read and wrote for many years: a man of letters and, in the best sense of the word, a dilettante.

While this book offers primarily a discussion of Peacock's novels, the discussion is prefaced by a brief summary, both of Peacock's life and of his other writings. The assumption is that these are relevant and helpful in an assessment of the novels. But there is another reason for such a discussion. Peacock was an enigmatic man. He was not only an intellectual and a writer, but also a public official, a practical and capable man of affairs. He could attack new inventions and with them the whole conception of mechanical 'progress', as unnecessary and harmful, and at the same time argue eloquently for the extension of steam navigation, about which he spoke as an expert.

His relationship to his age was complicated. For though he worshipped certain idols of the past, he tried to shatter many of the new idols of his times. In his writings and in his life, he was above all an iconoclast, speaking out against what he held to be false values and cant. Yet he lived, relatively prosperous and relatively happy, for more than eighty years.

## *Peacock's life*

In a memoir of his friend Shelley—written many years after Shelley's death—Peacock discussed his views on biography. Most biographical writing, he charged, is merely small gossip on a large scale, and detailed biographies are therefore at the least unfair, and probably injurious, to the subject. His attack is not primarily a moral one, nor was it new to his times. He felt, like many critics before him, that the subject of biography was entitled to privacy. If a man's writings are of value, then the writings ought to satisfy the public; and the public ought to concern itself with the public man. Perhaps to forestall his own biographers, Peacock left few records behind him. He managed to preserve then, even after death, the privacy that he guarded during his lifetime. Since he could not of course hide everything, we do have materials for a sketch.

He was born in 1785, the son of a glass merchant who died soon afterwards. Raised by his mother, who also served as his teacher, he grew up in London and in Chertsey, a village on the Thames. Apart from a brief period as a clerk, and another as a naval secretary (his family had naval connections), he remained unemployed until he was thirty-three, at which time he became a salaried officer in the East India House. The new position, which began formally in 1819, necessitated his moving to London. It also assured his financial security, a fact that must have been especially pleasant to Peacock because he had been accepting a regular stipend from Shelley, who could ill afford the generosity. Money enabled Peacock to marry, and his method of procuring a wife reflects the newly-made man of affairs. He wrote to Jane Gryffyd, a Welsh girl whom he had not seen for many years, and abruptly asked her hand. She demurred only slightly and they promptly married.

Peacock enjoyed London life. He kept spacious quarters. He frequented the theatre and the opera. For a period of four years he wrote regular music criticism (largely for The *Examiner*, the paper founded by Leigh Hunt). A capable public servant, he proved instrumental in extending steam navigation to the orient, and wrote an informed analysis of the problem for the *Edinburgh Review*. His position was an important one, and it became more so. He eventually succeeded James Mill as Examiner, one of the highest offices in the company. (He was himself succeeded by John Stuart Mill.) However much Peacock may have been gifted at administration, he seems not to have been enamoured of the daily routine. When he wrote examination papers during the preliminary screening for his position, the examiner's terse comment was: 'nothing superfluous and nothing wanting'. There is nothing superfluous and nothing wanting in his characterisation of that routine:

> From ten to eleven, ate a breakfast for seven:
> From eleven to noon, to begin 'twas too soon;
> From twelve to one, asked 'What's to be done?'
> From one to two, found nothing to do;
> From two to three began to foresee
> That from three to four would be a damned bore.

A 'damned bore' it may have been, but his job allowed him both the time and the money for his private interests, including the development of a large personal library. It enabled him, without serious conflict, to be what Macaulay called him, at once 'a clever fellow and a good scholar'.

Peacock did not live by a simple formula. He encountered many people in London. He dined regularly with Jeremy Bentham; he knew the Mills, Leigh Hunt, John Keats, William Hazlitt, and most of Shelley's wide acquaintance. Despite his having met many people, Peacock seems to have been intimate with few. Even with Shelley, a close friend for many years, he rarely put aside his reserve—and almost never in correspondence. Time and again Shelley wrote from Italy to ask what he was doing and writing. 'You are as secret,' he said to Peacock about *Nightmare Abbey*, 'as if the priest of Ceres had dictated its secret pages.' Apparently Peacock's closest confidante was his mother, to whom he is supposed to have read all his works, and whose tastes in literature in many cases became his own. For a number of years after her death (in 1833), he actually stopped writing.

Peacock enjoyed the city, but he preferred the country, where he could indulge his reclusive tastes. In the winter he wrote and read—two books at once according to one bewildered neighbour. In the summer he wandered and sailed (but rarely travelled; he never went farther than Wales and Scotland). A friend of Shelley described him as

> an idly inclined man; indeed he is professedly so in the summer; he owns he cannot apply himself to study, and thinks it more beneficial to him, as a human being, entirely to devote himself to the beauties of the season, while they last; he was only happy while out from morning till night.

This was Peacock as a young man, but the picture of indulgence, of the confirmed epicurean, devoting himself to nature's beauties 'while they last', is not far from Thackeray's characterisation of him, many years later, as 'a jolly old worldling'.

After retiring from the India House in 1856, Peacock moved permanently to his home in the country at Lower Halliford. He continued his lifelong habits of reading, especially in classical authors, and of devoting himself to whatever pleasures he could—'while they lasted'. He prepared recipes for his cook, though he never managed to collect them into a proposed cookbook, and he wrote, in addition to the final novel, *Gryll Grange*, which appeared when he was seventy-six, a few more essays and poems. Most of the poems of his last years were occasional. They bear comparison with many of the terse, epigrammatic verses of Walter Savage Landor. One of the last that he wrote, and one of the best, reveals the iconoclastic old man, still ironic, still impatient.

Instead of sitting wrapped up in flannel
  With rheumatism in every joint,
I wish I was in the English Channel,
  Just going round the Lizard Point,
All southward bound, with the seas before me,
  I should not care whether smooth or rough,
For then no visitors would call to bore me,
  Of whose 'good mornings' I have had enough.

By the time he wrote this poem, his visitors were of a new generation. Peacock had outlived the other writers of his own generation, in some cases—Keats, for example—by half a century. Seven years older than Shelley, Peacock lived over forty years after the death of his friend. He managed to have a long life without its usual trials—except that he outlived nearly all of his family. He may have looked upon himself, as he looked upon his friends and his times, with a wry skepticism, but he could make some compromise, or at least bear what was put upon him, and the worst that can be said about his life is that it was probably quiet. But again, if the external life seems uneventful, that is partly because we know little about it and partly because Peacock's intellectual and literary life proved the more important.

## *Peacock's writings*

Although he never published very much, Peacock wrote for a long time. His early verses are contemporary with those of the *Anti-Jacobin* and his final novel, *Gryll Grange*, appeared in 1861, the year Dickens published *Great Expectations*. Peacock not only bridged two literary generations, he also enjoyed two almost separate literary careers. He made as a boy of nine the following admission to his mother—as he wrote home from school:

> Dear Mother, I attempt to write you a letter,
> In verse, though in prose I could do it much better.

His prose did prove far better than his verse, as Peacock himself was to recognise, but he set out determined to be a poet. He wrote poetry almost exclusively for twenty years, then turned, almost as exclusively, to prose. The chronological division is partly a temperamental one—as between those rather dubious categories of romanticist and classicist—but not entirely so. His humorous novels always contain sentiment, however carefully disguised, and while some of his early poems read like exercises in melancholy, others are caustic and laughing. Still the division remains. Peacock wrote almost no prose before 1815, and he wrote no formal poetry after 1817; only the short ironic poems continued throughout his life.

Modern readers tend to characterise early nineteenth-century English poetry in terms of the innovations of Wordsworth, Coleridge, Shelley, Keats, and perhaps Byron; but a great part of the poetry of the time worked out fashionable eighteenth-century veins. Peacock's long poems had recognisable models in the late eighteenth century. He composed a Pindaric ode, *Palmyra* (1805); an excursionary poem, *The Genius of the Thames* (1810); and what, despite its title, amounts to a sustained hymn to dejection, *The Philosophy of Melancholy* (1812). In this last poem the man who was shortly to write boisterous comic novels asks a scornful question at the expense of laughter:

> Can the fantastic jest, the antic mirth,
> The laugh, that charms the grosser sons of earth,
> A joy so true, so softly sweet bestow,
> As genius gathers from the springs of woe?

Peacock's implied answer is clear; so is his self flattery; yet his 'genius' was to leave the 'springs of woe' far behind.

Actually Peacock's early years as a poet were not wholly devoted to the praise of dark-eyed melancholy. His earliest published poem, *The Monks of St. Mark* (published in 1803, apparently at his family's expense), is a rollicking narrative about a hedonistic assembly of monks. It concludes in an uproar akin to those that Peacock was to scatter through his novels:

> They reel'd back to their bowls, laugh'd at
> care and foul weather,
> And were shortly all under the table together.

*Sir Proteus* (1814) is a satiric portrait, though not a very good one, of Robert Southey, who had recently accepted the poet laureateship. *Sir Hornbook* and *The Round Table* are humorous and more or less educational poems for children. The best of Peacock's satiric and humorous poems, *Paper Money Lyrics*, were not written until 1825, but Peacock was not new to the art at that time. He also tried his hand at dramatic prologues, and even at verse dramas, two of which are boisterous farces. *The Dilettante* (1811?) and *The Three Doctors* (1812?) are set, like most of Peacock's novels, in country houses, where fast-talking caricatures and representatives of fads lock themselves in closets and argue over nothing. An especially impetuous character manages the following conclusion to an argument:

> This trigger, if I pull it
> Will emancipate a bullet
> That will set our quarrel right.

One has to assume that Peacock's earnest poems involved a pose. He did not suddenly develop a sense of humour and launch into his novels, for he wrote humorous works from the first. Perhaps the best explanation for his espousal of sober poetry is to be found in his conception of the poet and the function of poetry. For Peacock as a young man, poetry was a gentleman's art, a considered expression of formal ideas in a sufficiently exalted manner. The poet's task was to achieve the sublime by means of 'deep' thoughts and sounding phrases. When he wrote light verse and his novels, Peacock expressed himself with more freedom, in fact with an utter disregard of formal manner and lofty utterances. Indicative of his early commitment to the poetry, however, is the fact that two of his formal poems bore his name on the title page, whereas the humorous works all appeared anonymously.

At about the time that he wrote his last long poem, *Rhododaphne* (1818), Peacock seems to have realised, if not that his view of poetry was a narrow one, at least that he himself was not at his best in the kind of poems he had been writing. Ironically, *Rhododaphne* is a far better poem than any he had written before. Peacock wrote *Rhododaphne* after publishing *Headlong Hall* and *Melincourt*, his first two novels. While not humorous, it is—unlike the three earnest and rambling poems that preceded it—anything but mawkish. It is set in ancient Thessaly, a land associated with magic, and tells a story of love and enchantment. As a student of ancient erotic literature (according to one contemporary), Peacock delighted in his account of a beautiful witch, symbol of impure love, who seduces a quite willing young man through the course of seven cantos. *Rhododaphne* won deserving applause from Byron and Shelley. Edgar Allen Poe, unfamiliar with its author, called it 'brimful of music'.

*Rhododaphne* marked the end of Peacock's first literary career. After trying for years to win fame and money as a poet—and he was frank about his intent—he began only in his thirtieth year to write the works for which he is remembered, the comic novels that began with *Headlong Hall*. (Since these novels are our major interest, we will reserve any critical discussion of them for the following section.) Peacock wrote his novels over a span of forty-five years, and he finished only seven. Three were published within three years: *Headlong Hall* (1816); *Melincourt* (1817); and *Nightmare Abbey* (1818). A fourth, *Maid Marian*, started to take shape in 1818, but Peacock put it aside for several years when he began employment with the India House. It appeared finally in 1822, to be followed at intervals by *The Misfortunes of Elphin* (1829), *Crotchet Castle* (1831), and, many years later, by *Gryll Grange* (1861).

Soon after turning to the novel, he also turned to the essay, and he became during the next half century a literary reviewer, a music critic, and an occasional essayist. He published in 1820 the first and the best known of his essays, 'The Four Ages of Poetry', which is a kind of salty retirement speech at the end of Peacock's poetic career. An ironic diatribe against poetry, the essay begins with a pontifical announcement, a big critical spoof:

> Poetry, like the world, may be said to have four ages, but in a different order: the first age of poetry being the age of iron; the second, of gold; the third, of silver; and the fourth, of brass.

Poetry advances, achieves greatness, and declines, and at the very nadir of the cycle is the present age of poetry. Peacock speaks ironically, both in his denunciation of older poetry and in his argument that 'useful study' ought to supplant poetry in a 'polished and enlightened society'. He did not, for example, consider his society to be either polished or enlightened. But he is in earnest when he condemns 'our contemporary poetry'. Thus in the following passage he manages a crack at historians and philosophers as representatives of utilitarian optimism and at modern poets—the 'semi-barbarians in a civilised community'.

While the historian and the philosopher are advancing in, and accelerating, the progress of knowledge, the poet is wallowing in the rubbish of departed ignorance, and raking up the ashes of dead savages to find gewgaws and rattles for the grown babies of the age. Mr. Scott digs up the poachers and cattle-stealers of the ancient border. Lord Byron cruizes [sic] for thieves and pirates on the shores of the Morea and among the Greek islands. . . . Mr. Wordsworth picks up village legends from old women and sextons; and Mr. Coleridge, to the valuable information acquired from similar sources, superadds the dreams of crazy theologians and the mysticisms of German metaphysics, and favours the world with visions in verse, in which the quadruple elements of sexton, old woman, Jeremy Taylor, and Emanuel Kant, are harmonized into a delicious poetical compound.

This essay has some of the complex irony, some of the acerbity, that we associate with Swift, and Peacock here is at his closest to Swift. Elsewhere his attacks are usually, though not always, more genial and more balanced. Byron, for example, he considered self-indulgent and foolish, but he could praise *Don Juan* as a splendid poem. Shelley does not appear in 'The Four Ages', unless subsumed in the category of 'a few morbid ascetics', yet he responded to the essay—with the famous 'Defence of Poetry—as though he had been its chief victim.

Peacock's novels are rarely kind to either periodicals or periodical reviewers, and his first attempt at the essay, an unfinished attack on 'Fashionable Literature', indicted most aspects of periodical literature, including the demand for it. Yet Peacock himself contributed to several of the big periodicals, among them the *Westminister Review* and *Fraser's Magazine*. His topics included French comic romances, classical drama, books by Thomas Moore, the demolition of the old London Bridge, American politics, and cookery.

Few of Peacock's later essays shine like 'The Four Ages', but they are always informed, always wittily contentious. 'Gastronomy and Civilisation', for instance, sketches in a brief and opinionated way the progress of eating habits from the time of Homer, concluding with a partial lament about the decline of hospitality in modern England. It contains whimsicalities like the following:

We have recorded, as historical evidence, that the most incorruptible republicans were austere and abstemious; but it is still a question whether they would not have exerted a more beneficial influence, and have been better men, if they had moistened their throats with Madeira and enlarged their sympathies with grouse.

Peacock's essays make relatively clear not only what are disguised in his other writings, but also what are almost completely missing in his correspondence and in biographical accounts by contemporaries: namely his ideas, tastes, and prejudices. They point to his reverence for hospitality and conviviality, his respect for literary traditions and Lockean politics, his love of music, and his delight in rural —and female—beauty.

## *Reputation*

When Peacock died in 1866, few Englishmen noticed; few, perhaps, cared. Of the two known obituaries, only one associated him with 'the author of *Headlong Hall*', and it described him, paradoxically, as a writer of minor, of almost forgotten, classics, though a better writer than his reputation indicated. *The Times*, as if to acknowledge the other Peacock, the public man, merely remarked the passing of a retired India House officer. *Headlong Hall* had appeared fifty years before Peacock's death, and those who remembered the author (his name was known, despite the anonymous title page) must have wondered that he had lived so long.

Today the public man has been forgotten; the man of letters retains his equivocal position. To ask that always difficult because usually ironic question, 'Who now reads Peacock?' may offer a way of approaching his peculiar literary reputation. One point is clear: Peacock does have his readers. Rarely, if at all, have his works been out of print during the last seventy years. But they have never been popular.

Peacock wrote his novels at his leisure and as an amateur, and he packed into them, short as they are, a rather formidable part of his learning. He needs at times to be footnoted (he delighted in footnoting his own works) as much as any novelist. Part of his erudition may have been boasting, for Peacock almost gloated over the fact that he had avoided public schools, as well as Oxford and Cambridge, and he showed scant respect for the formal academic institutions of his time. Part of his erudition is sheer play: like Joyce and Mann in our own century, he happened to enjoy learned jokes. But part of his erudition is simply illusory and has to be explained in terms of how Peacock wrote, or what vehicle he chose. The satirist nearly always foxes the reader, lulling him into the comfortable illusion that he is different and exempt, a member of an enlightened group.

An ironist necessarily pays a toll; if he flatters some

readers, he excludes others from his point of view. Swift won royal dismay rather than the anticipated praise for his *Tale of a Tub*, and Peacock too has been misunderstood, sometimes by those who prided themselves on knowing him best. Even Shelley, long familiar with his work, completely mistook the import of 'The Four Ages of Poetry'. At other times, Shelley did understand Peacock's satire, and he enjoyed it too. His occasional bafflement, his delight in and distrust of Peacock's irony typifies the response of Peacock's contemporaries to his work. Some applauded his tolerance and wit. Some shouted in horror about his iconoclasm. But for the most part Peacock amused and was tolerated. He was, as he has remained, a favourite with many without being widely read.

Had Peacock enjoyed great popularity during his lifetime, like Byron, say, or Scott, he would have lived long enough to have seen the almost inevitable ebb and flow of reputation. But while there has been, especially in the last fifty years, a gradual swell of readers, and while Peacock's kind of writing has won a certain legitimacy, he has managed to rest in that somehow impossible category of 'forgotten classic'. If he is not, like Dickens, a widely known novelist, still Peacock is more than a curious memento of another age.

One clear sign that he has never been consigned to a literary grave is the interest other novelists have shown in his work. His country houses filled with eccentrics, his beautiful and emancipated young ladies, his emphasis on 'humorous' or monomaniacal types, his preference for dialogue—quick, intellectual, epigrammatic dialogue—over narrative: these are features that occur in many later writers. No doubt great novelists, like great poets—as T. S. Eliot said—do steal, whereas lesser writers make obvious borrowings. Some of Peacock's admirers are no longer remembered, and they are those—like W. H. Mallock—who most clearly aped his methods. But it is possible to trace Peacock's methods in writers who are very well known. Certainly Meredith learned a few points (and took a good many ideas) from Peacock, and possibly Dickens and Thackeray did too. In the twentieth century his most zealous students have been Evelyn Waugh and Aldous Huxley, who owe both their country houses and their format for brilliant talk to Peacock's novels. Kingsley Amis is another likely disciple.

That writers have continued to use Peacock is probably due—apart from the fact that he entertains—as much to his relevance for modern readers as for his literary format. He did, in a sense, write more for our times than for his own. Of course he satirised many areas of specifically nineteenth-century life, be it the implementation of gas lighting (which he thought, quite rightly, to be noxious), or the advent of mass travel. But if some of the specific targets have disappeared, the general conditions still prevail. People continue to dash mindlessly from place to place, running nowhere but away, and if they are no longer victims of gas lighting, they are certainly victims to a great deal of technology. Many of Peacock's polemics sound cranky or irresponsible; many did have merely local reference. Yet Peacock was one of few early nineteenth-century writers who could turn specific indictments into relevant general commentary. Unable to reconcile himself to the false optimism of progressive intellectual and social evolution, he anticipated—though with important differences—much of the 'absurd' comedy of the twentieth century.

It is however one feature of his satire or his comedy that seems particularly apt for the modern reader—and hence for the modern writer. Today we are nearly all specialists, specialists often enough against our will. Like Peacock's 'crotcheteering' characters we are unable to listen, unable to think, except according to our speciality. We may espouse tolerance, but we act together and alone like learned barbarians. We embody that brittleness, that inflexibility, of character that Henri Bergson thought the root of laughter—because the most anti-social, even anti-human, of traits. So Peacock looked forward, crystallising a tendency in his age that has become a chronic condition of our own. It is no small tribute to his powers that so many of his insights and his laughing judgments have withstood the test of time.

# *Scheme of extracts*

Although it would be desirable to introduce comments on his essays, the means of selection has been determined by persuasive facts. In the first place, Peacock's reputation rests on his novels, and with the exception of a few poems and essays, his novels contain his best work. Almost as important here, his other work remains difficult to come by, unless one has access to the Halliford Edition (see Selected Bibliography), whereas there are good and available editions of his novels.

Many approaches to fiction are possible, but here it has seemed appropriate, despite an occasional overlapping or repetition, to work from broad to specific and technical problems, and to include as many as possible of Peacock's literary techniques. The following categories offer a useful approach to his fiction:

1. Peacock's genre: his type of novel, with its sources and particular characteristics.
2. The novelistic world: the setting of his stories, and what the setting involves.
3. People and their talk: what kind of characters he draws, and what he does with dialogue.

4. Narrative and point of view: how he uses his narrator, and with what results.
5. Comedy: his humour and use of comic traditions.
6. Satire: his kind of attack, and his relation to some other writers of satire.

Of the following extracts from Peacock's novels, none is much longer than a few pages. Selection can, and usually does, involve questions of criticism: whether the author is distorted when quoted out of context; whether he is at his best in short passages, and so on. Peacock almost escapes these problems. In part because of his epigrammatic and quick dialogue, in part because of his kind of fiction, he makes his scenes, or his chapters—they are usually identical—curiously independent. Although they are of course related to what comes before and after, they are also self-sufficient enough to stand alone.

# *Peacock's genre*

In an essay on 'French Comic Romances', Peacock wrote that there are 'two very distinct classes of comic fictions: one in which the characters are abstractions or embodied classifications . . . and another in which the characters are individuals, and the events and the action those of actual life'. His own stories, like 'the fictions of Aristophanes, Petronius Arbiter, Rabelais, Swift, and Voltaire', are of the first class. In the second class Peacock puts novelists such as Fielding. Yet no writers—certainly not Fielding—really approximate 'actual life', for all literature necessarily involves abstractions and types. It is rather the illusion of the actual that characterises his second class, the apparent attempt on the author's part to hold up a mirror to the dusty road.

Even with this qualification, however, Peacock's distinction is more important as a clue to his own fiction than as a means of classifying his predecessors. He himself is uninterested in the illusion of the actual. This means that he excludes as a matter of course many things that have come to be associated with the novel, and it means that his works have to be approached in another way. If we expect from him the details of daily life and the psychological intricacies of individuals or families, we shall be disappointed. His novels contain nothing of passion or suffering; they explore only the absurd ramifications of absurd assumptions while excluding rigorously any topics not amenable to witty expression. They offer consistently the humorous distortions of burlesque and offer rarely, if at all, an attempt at verisimilitude. Peacock's stories may be thought of as intellectual games: difficult, in some ways inimitable, but with sharply defined rules and with boundaries close at hand.

If Peacock's novels all depict characters who are 'embodied classifications' and whose actions are not intended to be those of 'actual life', they include nevertheless at least two recognisable types of stories. *Headlong Hall, Melincourt, Crotchet Castle, Gryll Grange,* and usually also *Nightmare Abbey* are referred to as 'novels of talk' (or conversational novels) and *Maid Marian* and *The Misfortunes of Elphin* as 'romances'. These distinctions prove to be both helpful and limited as a means of identifying Peacock's type of narrative.

What apparently separates the two types is a matter of emphasis. The novels of talk have, as the phrase makes clear, conversation as their essential feature. Characters who typify various intellectual and literary fads meet together in isolated country retreats in order to talk about their preoccupations. If they are not talking, they are either walking, wooing, eating, or drinking, although they often manage all at once. The two romances differ from the novels of talk in several ways: they offer slightly more story; they are set in the past; they exhibit few spokesmen for intellectual fads; and they involve, proportionately, more narrative than dialogue. Both are akin to conventional romances in that they contain virtuous and featureless heroes and heroines, and that they progress somewhat casually along the lines of a quest. However they are recognisably Peacock's, and it can be argued that, despite the differences, they belong to the same literary genre as the other stories. In all seven books Peacock travesties the conventions of romance even as he imposes the conventions (the quest, the patient heroine, etc.) upon his narrative. Peacock always deflates his characters, chuckling at their follies. *Headlong Hall*, for example, concerns several pairs of lovers; the women are beautiful and a trifle absurd, the men articulate and thoroughly absurd. The story is minimal, but like that of the romances it is essentially a love story—or stories. Love, temporarily thwarted, at last triumphs. *Melincourt* is also a story of obstructed love; *Gryll Grange*, the final novel, works in a similar way, except that it and its characters are more complex.

*Nightmare Abbey* hovers somewhere between the novels of talk and the romances because it contains features of both. Like the novels of talk it *happens* in an indefinite near-past, and the guests of the abbey, who are recognisable caricatures of living men, come together for the related purposes of drinking and conversing. Like the romances it has more narrative than dialogue; it also has a recognisable plot, complete with 'recognitions' and 'reversals'. But the plot turns out to be burlesque, both of romance in general and, in particular, of Goethe's sentimental account of *The Sorrows of Young Werther*. Its complexity is simply that of the hero's difficulties in love. In *Nightmare Abbey* as in all the stories an outline of events would suggest romance, but Peacock's treatment of those events—his irony, humour, and burlesque—makes the vehicle satiric.

To say that Peacock experimented little with the format of his stories is not to suggest that his books are identical (though they are sometimes repetitious) or that they are of uniform quality. But certain materials, such as an emphasis on caricature, a simple, satiric plot with a comic resolution, an isolated rural setting, replete with music, food, and talk —these are present from first to last. It is probably no exaggeration to say that Peacock's works comprise the most homogenous group of novels in the language.

George Saintsbury, among others, preferred not to call them novels; he argued that tales or *contes* was better because he thought that Peacock's models were the eighteenth-century French writers of *contes*, Marmontel and Pigault le Brun. Peacock, who knew these writers, does at times approach their way of story-telling. Yet his talents and his interests are far more diverse, his satire more stringent. He is perhaps closer to the *conte philosophique*, that is, to the tales of Diderot and Voltaire, with whom he shared certain assumptions; but he did not share with them either a literary format or subject matter. Professor Saintsbury, eager like many other critics to put Peacock's fiction into an easy category, ignored differences in attempting to illustrate similarities. While Peacock may not have written novels like those of Fielding or Smollett, he also did not write tales in the manner of Pigault le Brun or Marmontel, at least in any complete sense. One therefore uses the term *novel*, whatever its inadequacies, for the simple reason that there is no clearly superior descriptive term.

Professor Saintsbury was quite right in pointing out that Peacock was indebted to various eighteenth-century French writers; Peacock was, however, equally indebted to writers of other times and other countries. There is always a difficulty in speaking about sources, and with Peacock there is the added difficulty that he borrowed from dozens of writers. A self-taught intellectual, he delighted in recondite allusions and verbal echoes. He takes a name like Facing-Both-Ways from John Bunyan and another, Doctor Opimian, from a Roman wine; one of his characters quotes a line out of Restoration comedy, another parodies an idea of Rousseau. This sort of borrowing is fairly easy to recognise (and Peacock often appends footnotes to make recognition easier), but it accounts for only a small part of his magpie approach to earlier literature. Adroitly, he puts together a jig-saw puzzle of apparently unrelated pieces, an amalgam of many kinds of writers. Some of these writers will be touched on in later sections, a few are relevant here.

In his list of comic writers quoted above—including Aristophanes, Rabelais, Swift, and Fielding—Peacock mentions the Roman author Petronius Arbiter. Petronius recurs in Peacock's novels: he is quoted, praised, and alluded to by a number of characters. His *Satyricon*, with its great banquet and its scathing satire, appealed to Peacock for various reasons, perhaps the most important of which was its literary genre. Peacock's tone is different from that of Petronius, and his interests are different too, but Peacock probably borrowed from Petronius—or from his followers—a general means of presenting his material. Petronius wrote what has come to be called Menippean satire (after Menippus, a Latin writer whose works have been lost but who probably wrote a kind of angry sermon). Satire owes its name to the word *satura* or medley: it has been from the first a mixed genre, related to but also different from comedy. Hence perhaps some of the difficulties involved in its criticism. By Menippean satire is meant a form of narrative satire having few formal restrictions, a loose and inclusive mixture of prose and verse, narrative and dialogue. In the hands of Rabelais (whom Peacock drew upon time and time again), Menippean satire became a formidable hodge-podge of laughter and wit; in the hands of Robert Burton (whose *Anatomy of Melancholy* is a closely related work), it became a vehicle encompassing most of the learning of the time. Peacock does not write like Burton and Rabelais, although he borrowed something from both. Where they included, he excluded; where they filled out, he refined. While, like Rabelais, he may delight in digression, unlike Rabelais he ties up loose ends, and by insisting upon a formal, comic resolution, he ignores the dictates of satire.

The foregoing description may sound a little like Polonius's classification of dramatic types. Just what have we established? We have shown in a general way that Peacock's fiction includes verbal echoes and literary characteristics from various sources; that his books are—the differences between the romances and the novels of talk notwithstanding—very closely related; and that because of his kind of book Peacock offers another kind of entertainment than is found in the novels of, say, Fielding or Scott. At the same time Peacock did know and in part emulated several English novelists. What he did, in short, was to return to one of the original sources of the novel—Menippean satire—and to impose upon that loose and malleable genre certain conventions from other dramatic and fictional forms. These points will be clarified in later sections.

The second of Peacock's comic historical romances, *The Misfortunes of Elphin* takes place in legendary or pre-historic Wales. Peacock had long been interested in things Welsh. His poem *The Philosophy of Melancholy* (1812) describes the perverse pleasure to be gained from melancholy communion with Cambrian mountains (while hinting at the attractions of Cambrian women). *Headlong Hall* is set in a rugged part of Wales; so are parts of the unfinished 'Calidore' (1816). Peacock himself took several extended trips to Wales and extolled the country, though not the people, in his correspondence.

*Elphin* represents more than an affection for Wales. It

is the product of actual researches, the model for which was probably Thomas Gray, whom Peacock parodies more than once in the course of the story. Yet he needed no specific impetus, since antiquarians had been interested in Wales for a generation or more. *Elphin* yokes together several ancient legends: that of the poet Taliesin (real, if not nominal hero of the story), that of King Arthur, and that of Prince Seithenyn. Peacock gives neither Elphin, Taliesin, nor Arthur particularly clear features, but he makes Seithenyn into the most bibulous, the most Falstaffian of all his characters. J. B. Priestley calls Seithenyn one of the great English comic characters.

In the following scene Prince Elphin, about to inherit his kingdom (which is about to be inundated by the sea), arrives with a companion at Seithenyn's palace, in a fruitless effort to induce the 'lord of the embankment' to begin reforms.

## I

### *'The Drunkenness of Seithenyn'*

> The three immortal drunkards of the isle of Britain: Ceraint of Essyllwg; Gwrtheyrn Gwrtheneau; and Seithenyn ap Seithyn Saidi.
>
> *Triads of the Isle of Britain.*

The sun had sunk beneath the waves when they reached the castle of Seithenyn. The sound of the harp and the song saluted them as they approached it. As they entered the great hall, which was already blazing with torchlight, they found his highness, and his highness's household, convincing themselves and each other with wine and wassail, of the excellence of their system of virtual superintendence; and the following jovial chorus broke on the ears of the visitors:

### THE CIRCLING OF THE MEAD HORNS

Fill the blue horn, the blue buffalo horn:
Natural is mead in the buffalo horn:
As the cuckoo in spring, as the lark in the morn,
So natural is mead in the buffalo horn.

As the cup of the flower to the bee when he sips,
Is the full cup of mead to the true Briton's lips:
From the flower-cups of summer, on the field and on tree,
Our mead cups are filled by the vintager bee.

Seithenyn[1] ap Seithyn, the generous, the bold,
Drinks the wine of the stranger from vessels of gold;[2]
But we from the horn, the blue silver-rimmed horn,
Drink the ale and the mead in our fields that were born.

The ale-froth is white, and the mead sparkles bright;
They both smile apart, and with smiles they unite:[3]
The mead from the flower, and the ale from the corn,
Smile, sparkle, and sing in the buffalo horn.

The horn, the blue horn, cannot stand on its tip;
Its path is right on from the hand to the lip:
Though the bowl and the wine-cup our tables adorn,
More natural the draught from the buffalo horn.

But Seithenyn ap Seithyn, the generous, the bold,
Drinks the bright-flowing wine from the far-gleaming
gold:
The wine, in the bowl by his lip that is worn,
Shall be glorious as mead in the buffalo horn.

The horns circle fast, but their fountains will last,
As the stream passes ever, and never is past:
Exhausted so quickly, replenished so soon,
They wax and they wane like the horns of the moon.

[1] The accent is on the second syllable: Seithényn. [Peacock.]

[2] Gwin . . . . o eur . . . . ANEURIN. [Peacock.]

[3] The mixture of ale and mead made *bradawd*, a favourite drink of the Ancient Britons. [Peacock.]

Fill high the blue horn, the blue buffalo horn;
Fill high the long silver-rimmed buffalo horn:
While the roof of the hall by our chorus is torn,
Fill, fill to the brim, the deep silver-rimmed horn.

Elphin and Teithrin stood some time on the floor of the hall before they attracted the attention of Seithenyn, who, during the chorus, was tossing and flourishing his golden goblet. The chorus had scarcely ended when he noticed them, and immediately roared aloud, 'You are welcome all four.'

Elphin answered, 'We thank you: we are but two.'

'Two or four,' said Seithenyn, 'all is one. You are welcome all. When a stranger enters, the custom in other places is to begin by washing his feet. My custom is, to begin by washing his throat. Seithenyn ap Seithyn Saidi bids you welcome.'

Elphin, taking the wine-cup, answered, 'Elphin ap Gwythno Garanhir thanks you.'

Seithenyn started up. He endeavoured to straighten himself into perpendicularity, and to stand steadily on his legs. He accomplished half his object by stiffening all his joints but those of his ancles, and from these the rest of his body vibrated upwards with the inflexibility of a bar. After thus oscillating for a time, like an inverted pendulum, finding that the attention requisite to preserve his rigidity absorbed all he could collect of his dissipated energies, and that he required a portion of them for the management of his voice, which he felt a dizzy desire to wield with peculiar steadiness in the presence of the son of the king, he suddenly relaxed the muscles that perform the operation of sitting, and dropped into his chair like a plummet. He then, with a gracious gesticulation, invited Prince Elphin to take his seat on his right hand, and proceeded to compose himself into a dignified attitude, throwing his body back into the left corner of his chair, resting his left elbow on its arm and his left cheekbone on the middle of the back of his left hand, placing his left foot on a footstool, and stretching out his right leg as straight and as far as his position allowed. He had thus his right hand at liberty, for the ornament of his eloquence and the conduct of his liquor.

Elphin seated himself at the right hand of Seithenyn. Teithrin remained at the end of the hall: on which Seithenyn exclaimed, 'Come on, man, come on. What, if you be not the son of a king, you are the guest of Seithenyn ap Seithyn Saidi. The most honourable place to the most honourable guest, and the next most honourable place to the next most honourable guest; the least honourable guest above the most honourable inmate; and, where there are but two guests, be the most honourable who he may, the least honourable of the two is next in honour to the most honourable of the two, because they are no more but two; and, where there are only two, there can be nothing between. Therefore sit, and drink. GWIN O EUR: wine from gold.'

Elphin motioned Teithrin to approach, and sit next to him.

Prince Seithenyn, whose liquor was 'his eating and his drinking solely,'[4] seemed to measure the gastronomy of his guests by his own; but his groom of the pantry thought the strangers might be disposed to eat, and placed before them a choice of provision, on which Teithrin ap Tathral did vigorous execution.

'I pray your excuses,' said Seithenyn, 'my stomach is weak, and I am subject to dizziness in the head, and my memory is not so good as it was, and my faculties of attention are somewhat impaired, and I would dilate more upon the topic, whereby you should hold me excused, but I am troubled with a feverishness and parching of the mouth, that very much injures my speech, and impedes my saying all I would say, and will say before I have done, in token

[4] Quoted from Beaumont and Fletcher's *The Scornful Lady*.

of my loyalty and fealty to your highness and your highness's house. I must just moisten my lips, and I will then proceed with my observations. Cupbearer, fill.'

'Prince Seithenyn,' said Elphin, 'I have visited you on a subject of deep moment. Reports have been brought to me, that the embankment, which has been so long intrusted to your care, is in a state of dangerous decay.'

'Decay,' said Seithenyn, 'is one thing, and danger is another. Every thing that is old must decay. That the embankment is old, I am free to confess; that it is somewhat rotten in parts, I will not altogether deny; that it is any the worse for that, I do most sturdily gainsay. It does its business well: it works well: it keeps out the water from the land, and it lets in the wine upon the High Commission of Embankment. Cupbearer, fill. Our ancestors were wiser than we: they built it in their wisdom; and, if we should be so rash as to try to mend it, we should only mar it.'

'The stonework,' said Teithrin, 'is sapped and mined: the piles are rotten, broken, and dislocated: the floodgates and sluices are leaky and creaky.'

'That is the beauty of it,' said Seithenyn. 'Some parts of it are rotten, and some parts of it are sound.'

'It is well,' said Elphin, 'that some parts are sound: it were better that all were so.'

'So I have heard some people say before,' said Seithenyn; 'perverse people, blind to venerable antiquity: that very unamiable sort of people, who are in the habit of indulging their reason. But I say, the parts that are rotten give elasticity to those that are sound: they give them elasticity, elasticity, elasticity. If it were all sound, it would break by its own obstinate stiffness: the soundness is checked by the rottenness, and the stiffness is balanced by the elasticity. There is nothing so dangerous as innovation. See the waves in the equinoctial storms, dashing and clashing, roaring and pouring, spattering and battering, rattling and battling against it. I would not be so presumptuous as to say, I could build any thing that would stand against them half an hour; and here this immortal old work, which God forbid the finger of modern mason should bring into jeopardy, this immortal work has stood for centuries, and will stand for centuries more if we let it alone. It is well: it works well: let well alone. Cupbearer, fill. It was half rotten when I was born, and that is a conclusive reason why it should be three parts rotten when I die.'[5]

The whole body of the High Commission roared approbation.

'And after all,' said Seithenyn, 'the worst that could happen would be the overflow of a springtide, for that was the worst that happened before the embankment was thought of; and, if the high water should come in, as it did before, the low water would go out again, as it did before. We should be no deeper in it than our ancestors were, and we could mend as easily as they could make.'

'The level of the sea,' said Teithrin, 'is materially altered.'

'The level of the sea!' exclaimed Seithenyn. 'Who ever heard of such a thing as altering the level of the sea? Alter the level of that bowl of wine before you, in which, as I sit here, I see a very ugly reflection of your very goodlooking face. Alter the level of that: drink up the reflection: let me see the face without the reflection, and leave the sea to level itself.'

'Not to level the embankment,' said Teithrin.

'Good, very good,' said Seithenyn. 'I love a smart saying, though it hits at me. But, whether yours is a smart saying or no, I do not very clearly see; and, whether it hits at me or no, I do not very sensibly feel. But all is one. Cupbearer, fill.'

*The Misfortunes of Elphin*, ch. II

Like Scott, from whom he probably took the idea of

[5] Seithenyn has been identified with various political figures of the time (shortly before the 1832 Reform Bill), but he satirises extreme conservatism of all times.

writing a romance, Peacock assumes a detached and ironic manner in discussing his characters. Scott's Wamba, in *Ivanhoe*, bears the same relationship to the narrator as Seithenyn does to Peacock's narrator. Both authors, rather like benevolent uncles, tell their stories with amused tolerance. But Scott's humour never becomes too insistent, never usurps the 'serious' story. His humorous scenes are interludes, and his irony is that of detachment. Peacock, on the other hand, maintains his humour by continually undercutting his characters. Even the heroes are subject to mockery, and the narrator rarely says anything that is not tongue-in-cheek.

In the passage from *Elphin*, the two young men purportedly visit Seithenyn on a serious mission. After all, their country stands in imminent danger of submersion: they must persuade the lord of the embankment (who embodies those who oppose any reform with any and all arguments) to do *something*. Yet Peacock burlesques their mission, and he makes Seithenyn, who ought to be a knave, into a sympathetic buffoon.

Peacock may also have learned from Scott, and from other writers of romance, how to incorporate songs into his narrative. The practice, common to Menippean satire as well as romance, fell into disuse among the 'realistic' novelists of the eighteenth century, so much so, that not even Scott could make it popular again. Peacock's songs are worth commenting on. Many of the best occur in his novels, and they are, characteristically, light, laughing, and short. They range from love lyrics to nonsense verses. 'The Circling of the Mead Horn' may not be especially noteworthy, but *Elphin* does include one of the finest; Peacock introduces it as 'the quintessence of all the war-songs that ever were written, and the sum and substance of all the appetencies, tendencies, and consequences of military glory'. The first stanza of 'The War-Song of Dinas Vawr' runs as follows:

> The mountain sheep are sweeter,
> But the valley sheep are fatter;
> We therefore deemed it meeter
> To carry off the latter.
> We made an expedition;
> We met a host, and quelled it;
> We forced a strong position,
> And killed the men who held it.

'The War-Song' is Peacock's own, whereas 'The Circling of the Mead Horns' and most of the other songs in *Elphin* are translations from the Welsh, or at most verse renderings.

In *Elphin*, the songs, as in Scott's novels, provide musical pauses without much influencing the narrative. Elsewhere, and most conspicuously in *Melincourt* and *Maid Marian*, they become a means both of showing-off the heroines and restoring harmony. It was appropriate that *Maid Marian* was adapted for the theatre, for it contains many of the features of light opera—including a flimsy plot. Some critics think that Peacock anticipated, if he did not directly influence, songs of Gilbert and Sullivan. Certainly his war song is as fine a lyric as many of Gilbert's, and as absurdly satiric, too, as the poems of Edward Lear and Lewis Carroll.

In *Crotchet Castle* Peacock returned from the two 'historical' romances to his earlier format. Again he set his story on a secluded rural estate, there to introduce an assortment of 'crotcheteers'. As the story progresses, the group sheds its most absurd characters, or at least its less gregarious ones, and becomes, as is usual in Peacock's stories, more or less congenial. At the close, all is well: the various lovers have been united, and the outside world has been exposed as materialistic, urbanised, and full of cant. The following is the second chapter of the novel, when the talk is getting under way. Here, typically, Peacock retires as narrator in favour of other voices.

2

*'The March of Mind'*

> Quoth Ralpho: nothing but the abuse
> Of human learning you produce.—BUTLER.[6]

'God bless my soul, sir!' exclaimed the Reverend Doctor Folliott, bursting, one fine May morning, into the breakfast-room at Crotchet Castle, 'I am out of all patience with this march of mind. Here has my house been nearly burned down, by my cook taking it into her head to study hydrostatics, in a sixpenny tract, published by the Steam Intellect Society, and written by a learned friend who is for doing all the world's business as well as his own, and is equally well qualified to handle every branch of human knowledge.[7] I have a great abomination of this learned friend; as author, lawyer, and politician, he is *triformis*, like Hecate: and in every one of his three forms he is *bifrons*, like Janus; the true Mr. Facing-both-ways of Vanity Fair. My cook must read his rubbish in bed; and as might naturally be expected, she dropped suddenly fast asleep, overturned the candle, and set the curtains in a blaze. Luckily, the footman went into the room at the moment, in time to tear down the curtains and throw them into the chimney, and a pitcher of water on her nightcap extinguished her wick: she is a greasy subject, and would have burned like a short mould.'

The reverend gentleman exhaled his grievance without

[6] From Samuel Butler's *Hudibras*.

[7] Peacock is referring to Lord Brougham and The Society for the Diffusion of Useful Knowledge (founded 1825).

looking to the right or to the left; at length, turning on his pivot, he perceived that the room was full of company, consisting of young Crotchet and some visitors whom he had brought from London. The Reverend Doctor Folliott was introduced to Mr. Mac Quedy,[8] the economist; Mr. Skionar,[9] the transcendental poet; Mr. Firedamp, the meteorologist; and Lord Bossnowl, son of the Earl of Foolincourt, and member for the borough of Rogueingrain.

The divine took his seat at the breakfast-table, and began to compose his spirits by the gentle sedative of a large cup of tea, the demulcent of a well-buttered muffin, and the tonic of a small lobster.

THE REV. DR. FOLLIOTT

You are a man of taste, Mr. Crotchet. A man of taste is seen at once in the array of his breakfast-table. It is the foot of Hercules, the far-shining face of the great work, according to Pindar's doctrine: *ἀρχομένου ἔργου, πρόσωπον χρὴ θέμεν τηλαυγές*.[10] The breakfast is the *πρόσωπον* of the great work of the day. Chocolate, coffee, tea, cream, eggs, ham, tongue, cold fowl,—all these are good, and bespeak good knowledge in him who sets them forth: but the touchstone is fish: anchovy is the first step, prawns and shrimps the second; and I laud him who reaches even to these: potted char and lampreys are the third, and a fine stretch of progression; but lobster is, indeed, matter for a May morning, and demands a rare combination of knowledge and virtue in him who sets it forth.

MR. MAC QUEDY

Well, sir, and what say you to a fine fresh trout, hot and

[8] Quasi Mac Q. E. D., son of a demonstration. [Peacock.]

[9] ΣKlas ONAP. *Umbræ somnium.* [Peacock.] He probably has Coleridge in mind. See p. 51 ff.

[10] Far-shining be the face
Of a great work begun.—Pindar. *Ol.* vi. [Peacock.]

dry, in a napkin? or a herring out of the water into the frying pan, on the shore of Loch Fyne?

THE REV. DR. FOLLIOTT

Sir, I say every nation has some eximious virtue; and your country is pre-eminent in the glory of fish for breakfast. We have much to learn from you in that line at any rate.

MR. MAC QUEDY

And in many others, sir, I believe. Morals and metaphysics, politics and political economy, the way to make the most of all the modifications of smoke; steam, gas, and paper currency; you have all these to learn from us; in short, all the arts and sciences. We are the modern Athenians.[11]

THE REV. DR. FOLLIOTT

I, for one, sir, am content to learn nothing from you but the art and science of fish for breakfast. Be content, sir, to rival the Bœotians, whose redeeming virtue was in fish, touching which point you may consult Aristophanes and his scholiast, in the passage of Lysistrata, *ἀλλ' ἄφελε τὰς ἐγχέλεις*,[12] and leave the name of Athenians to those who have a sense of the beautiful, and a perception of metrical quantity.

MR. MAC QUEDY

Then, sir, I presume you set no value on the right principles of rent, profit, wages, and currency?

[11] Like many of his countrymen, Peacock enjoyed witticism at the expense of the Scots. The claim that Scotland, or more specifically, Edinburgh, was the Modern Athens seems to have been common, and it was not as ill-founded as Peacock's satire suggests.

[12] Calonice wishes destruction to all Bœotians. Lysistrata answers, '*Except the eels.*' Lysistrata, 36. [Peacock.] One of numerous references to Aristophanes.

THE REV. DR. FOLLIOTT

My principles, sir, in these things are, to take as much as I can get, and to pay no more than I can help. These are every man's principles, whether they be the right principles or no. There, sir, is political economy in a nutshell.

MR. MAC QUEDY

The principles, sir, which regulate production and consumption, are independent of the will of any individual as to giving or taking, and do not lie in a nutshell by any means.

THE REV. DR. FOLLIOTT

Sir, I will thank you for a leg of that capon.

LORD BOSSNOWL

But, sir, by the by, how came your footman to be going into your cook's room? It was very providential to be sure, but—

THE REV. DR. FOLLIOTT

Sir, as good came of it, I shut my eyes, and asked no questions. I suppose he was going to study hydrostatics, and he found himself under the necessity of practising hydraulics.

*Crotchet Castle*, ch. II

The motto for the 'March of Mind' comes appropriately from Samuel Butler, whose *Hudibras* was one of Peacock's favourite comic poems. Peacock like Butler delights in characters with fixed opinions, or with fixations. The Reverend Doctor Folliott, for example, is a dogmatic hedonist, whom Peacock has characterised in the foregoing chapter by a description of the origin of his name. Folliott's 'indefatigable pair of lungs' 'gave occasion to some etymologists to ring changes on his name, and to decide that it was derived from Follis Optimus, softened through an Italian medium into Folle Ottimo, contracted poetically into Folleotto, and elided Anglicé into Folliott, signifying a first-rate pair of bellows'. Mr. Mac Quedy, the 'son of a demonstration', is probably based upon a particular Scot, but he serves generally as a representative Scot and as a utilitarian. Missing from the breakfast is another man of Scottish derivation, Mr. Crotchet Sr., whose father 'had walked up to London on a commercial adventure, with all his surplus capital, not very neatly tied up in a not very clean handkerchief'. The squire is a member of the *nouveaux riches*—like Trimalchio in the *Satyricon*—and Peacock satirises his ostentatious consumption and his desire for 'philosophical' companionship. Because of his 'inborn love of disputation' and his ready hospitality, 'a numerous detachment from the advanced guard of the "march of intellect", often marched down to Crotchet Castle.'

Crotchet's abundant breakfast table may be an Englished version of Petronius's Roman banquet, complete with its representative types and appropriate (that is, much more restrained) manners. There were however other banquets, some modern, some ancient, which seem relevant to 'The March of Mind' and to many other of Peacock's table scenes. Peacock admired, for example, Plato's dialogues, and of the dialogues he admired especially the *Symposium*. He creates modern equivalents for Sir Hudibras rather than for Socrates, but he does present his characters with ample food and beverage and with topics for conversation. In this case, the frame of the chapter is the story of Folliott's maid, who has been victimised (in Folliott's version) by the Steam Intellect Society and the Learned Friend. The frame is a slight one of course. It gives Folliott a means of opening the talk—as he bursts into the room—and it enables the author to end the chapter with a bad pun and an expected joke. Between the introduction and the conclusion the characters range freely over other topics. Plato enters the conversation later in the story; both Folliott and Crotchet use him as an authority and ascribe his neglect in nineteenth-century England to the fact that modern society lacks all the virtues that he espoused.

Another writer of a symposium was Athenaeus, a man who actually collected conversations of great men and fitted them loosely together, as *The Sophists at Dinner*, into a dialogue. Peacock prided himself on knowing Athenaeus, and he lets various characters, including Folliott, quote his work with approval. To the extent that his characters represent living men (such as Lord Brougham), Peacock might be writing a parody of Athenaeus's book.

Various other writers of Peacock's time interested themselves in dialogues and symposia. Horne Tooke and William Drummond, both forgotten writers, are referred to several times in Peacock's novels. Peacock rarely mentions Walter Savage Landor, but Landor is, of Peacock's contemporaries, in some ways the closest to his work. Landor wrote the *Imaginary Conversations*, in which he posited either a topic or a situation and 'imagined' a dialogue between certain literary or historical characters. Landor's dialogues are more formal than Peacock's, and much less farcical. Both writers shared, nevertheless, their love of talk and of ideas; both looked back to classical times for the authority to judge their own; and both felt at odds with mechanistic and 'progressive' nineteenth-century England, with what Peacock here calls 'the march of mind'.

The illusion in this as in many of Peacock's chapters is that they are composed entirely of dialogue. In fact the narrator introduces the scene, interjects comment, and manages to guide the reader's judgment. This is a matter to be taken up later.

## *The novelistic world*

'Every novelist,' wrote Joseph Conrad, 'must begin by creating for himself a world, great or little, in which he can honestly believe.' The important word here is *create*, for Conrad ignores the conventional idea of a writer choosing a particular *locale*—or, to make the process yet more passive, his being given that *locale*. Conrad does of course seem to have more than setting in mind. It is only in a limited sense that he himself creates the sea within his own novels; what he does create is the combination of sea, ship, and men, the sum of which becomes his world. But this is still to construe world as a kind of mechanical stage. For Conrad the word involves an entire moral order—or lack of order; it involves finally the re-setting of men in a re-created world, a world with its own laws and its own conventions.

Conrad's is a 'great' world. It includes so much that many readers confuse the simulated with the actual, and Conrad's art, for them, becomes a muddled version of life. Few readers would make the same confusion when reading Peacock. His is a 'little' world with an artificial setting or stage; its laws are the traditional laws of satire and comedy. Peacock prefers the stylised, the caricatured, the restricted.

If there is any difficulty in appreciating his novels, it lies in the fact that most modern readers are used to 'realism' and may be impatient with a writer for whom realism was not the end of all art but merely a convention of one kind of fiction. Whether Peacock's was a world in which he could 'honestly believe' must remain a moot question, largely because Peacock never mentioned this kind of topic, but also because he was uninterested in the essentially romantic assumptions about sincerity in art. Conrad's novelistic realism and 'honesty' would probably have bored him, as not showing enough artifice. Peacock does nevertheless create his world, and it is a comic world, in which actions and dialogue are caught, not in a conventional, but in a burlesquing and distorting mirror.

Usually Peacock sets his characters in a country house —more specifically, at table. His setting is, in spite of the outside satiric references, almost hermetically intact, for whether he describes Sherwood Forest in an idealised twelfth century or Wales in the nineteenth century, he creates the same rural and isolated world within a world, far from the cares and sufferings of ordinary life.

For certain features of his setting—if not for its distinctive quality—Peacock seems indebted to a number of eighteenth-century novelists, Fielding and Sterne among them. Thomas Amory (*The Adventures of John Buncle*), Richard Graves (*Columella*), and Robert Bage (most notably in *Mount Henneth* and *Hermsprong*) had introduced their characters into remote and beautiful regions, there to let them talk. Scott, too, may have been in Peacock's mind: some descriptions in *Headlong Hall* parallel descriptions of Scottish scenery in *Waverley* (1814). Peacock's descriptions can be as vague as Scott's or as precise in a similarly mannered and picturesque way. Scenery is occasionally central to his stories, though it generally serves as an idealised backdrop, akin to the painted scenes in operatic productions that Peacock greatly admired.

In *Headlong Hall* Peacock builds Squire Headlong's estate in the Welsh mountains. Only the Squire and his sister are in any way Welsh, however, for it was the countryside itself and the absence of *ordinary* people, that delighted Peacock. He imports into the imaginary estate the imaginary representatives of various people, fads, and ideas, and he severs any connection they might be expected to have with the outside world. Peacock's houses are, in their isolation, analagous to Conrad's ships; but here are no storms or struggles. The guests arrive in December in order to enjoy with Headlong the Christmas festivities.

## 3

### *'The Mail'*

The ambiguous light of a December morning, peeping through the windows of the Holyhead mail, dispelled the soft visions of the four insides, who had slept, or seemed to sleep, through the first seventy miles of the road, with as much comfort as may be supposed consistent with the jolting of the vehicle, and an occasional admonition to *remember the coachman,* thundered through the open door, accompanied by the gentle breath of Boreas, into the ears of the drowsy traveller.

A lively remark, that *the day was none of the finest,* having elicited a repartee of *quite the contrary,* the various knotty points of meteorology, which usually form the exordium of an English conversation, were successively discussed and exhausted; and, the ice being thus broken, the colloquy rambled to other topics, in the course of which it appeared, to the surprise of every one, that all four, though perfect strangers to each other, were actually bound to the same point, namely, Headlong Hall, the seat of the ancient and honourable family of the Headlongs, of the vale of Llanberis, in Caernarvonshire. This name may appear at first sight not to be truly Cambrian, like those of the Rices, and Prices, and Morgans, and Owens, and Williamses, and Evanses, and Parrys, and Joneses; but, nevertheless, the Headlongs claim to be not less genuine derivatives from the antique branch of Cadwallader than any of the last named multiramified families. They claim, indeed, by one account, superior antiquity to all of them, and even to Cadwallader himself; a tradition having been handed down in Headlong Hall for some few thousand years, that the founder of the family was preserved in the deluge on the summit of Snowdon, and took the name of Rhaiader, which signifies a *waterfall*, in consequence of his having accompanied the water in its descent or diminution, till he found himself comfortably seated on the rocks of Llanberis. But, in later days, when commercial bagsmen began to scour the country, the ambiguity of the sound induced his descendants to drop the suspicious denomination of *Riders*, and translate the word into English; when, not being well pleased with the sound of the *thing*, they substituted that of the *quality*, and accordingly adopted the name *Headlong*, the appropriate epithet of waterfall.

I cannot tell how the truth may be:
I say the tale as 't was said to me.[1]

The present representative of this ancient and dignified house, Harry Headlong, Esquire, was, like all other Welsh squires, fond of shooting, hunting, racing, drinking, and other such innocent amusements, *μειζονς δ' αλλου τινος*, as Menander expresses it. But, unlike other Welsh squires, he had actually suffered certain phenomena, called books, to find their way into his house; and, by dint of lounging over them after dinner, on those occasions when he was

[1] From Sir Walter Scott's *Lay of the Last Minstrel*. Peacock delighted in spurious 'tales' of ancestry.

compelled to take his bottle alone, he became seized with a violent passion to be thought a philosopher and a man of taste; and accordingly set off on an expedition to Oxford, to inquire for other varieties of the same genera, namely, men of taste and philosophers; but, being assured by a learned professor that there were no such things in the University, he proceeded to London, where, after beating up in several booksellers' shops, theatres, exhibition-rooms, and other resorts of literature and taste, he formed as extensive an acquaintance with philosophers and dilettanti as his utmost ambition could desire; and it now became his chief wish to have them all together in Headlong Hall, arguing, over his old Port and Burgundy, the various knotty points which had puzzled his pericranium. He had, therefore, sent them invitations in due form to pass their Christmas at Headlong Hall; which invitations the extensive fame of his kitchen fire had induced the greater part of them to accept; and four of the chosen guests had, from different parts of the metropolis, ensconced themselves in the four corners of the Holyhead mail.

These four persons were, Mr. Foster,[2] the perfectibilian; Mr. Escot,[3] the deteriorationist; Mr. Jenkison,[4] the statu-

[2] Foster, quasi Φωστηρ,—from φαος and τηρεω, lucem servo, conservo, observo, custodio,—one who watches over and guards the light; a sense in which the word is often used amongst us, when we speak of fostering a flame. [Peacock.] Foster is based, in part, on Shelley, See p. 51. But Shelley, like Mr. Escot, was a vegetarian.

[3] Escot, quasi ες σκοτον, *in tenebras*, scilicet, intuens; one who is always looking into the dark side of the question. [Peacock.]

[4] Jenkison: This name may be derived from αιεν εξ ισων, *semper ex œqualibus*—scilicet, mensuris, omnia, metiens: one who from equal measures divides and distributes all things: one who from equal measures can always produce arguments on both sides of a question, with so much nicety and exactness, as to keep the said question eternally pending, and the balance of the controversy perpetually in statu quo. By an aphæresis of the α, an elision of the second ε, and an easy and natural mutation of ξ into κ, the derivation of this name proceeds according to the strictest principles of etymology: αιεν εξ ισων—Ιεν εξ ισων—Ιεν εκ ισων—Ιεν 'κ ισων—Ιενκισων—Ienkison—Jenkison. [Peacock.]

quo-ite; and the Reverend Doctor Gaster,[5] who, though of course neither a philosopher nor a man of taste, had so won on the Squire's fancy, by a learned dissertation on the art of stuffing a turkey, that he concluded no Christmas party would be complete without him.

The conversation among these illuminati soon became animated; and Mr. Foster, who, we must observe, was a thin gentleman, about thirty years of age, with an aquiline nose, black eyes, white teeth, and black hair—took occasion to panegyrize the vehicle in which they were then travelling, and observed what remarkable improvements had been made in the means of facilitating intercourse between distant parts of the kingdom: he held forth with great energy on the subject of roads and railways, canals and tunnels, manufactures and machinery: 'In short,' said he, 'every thing we look on attests the progress of mankind in all the arts of life, and demonstrates their gradual advancement towards a state of unlimited perfection.'

Mr. Escot, who was somewhat younger than Mr. Foster, but rather more pale and saturnine in his aspect, here took up the thread of the discourse, observing, that the proposition just advanced seemed to him perfectly contrary to the true state of the case: 'for,' said he, 'these improvements, as you call them, appear to me only so many links in the great chain of corruption, which will soon fetter the whole human race in irreparable slavery and incurable wretchedness: your improvements proceed in a simple ratio, while the factitious wants and unnatural appetites they engender proceed in a compound one; and thus one generation acquires fifty wants, and fifty means of supplying them are invented, which each in its turn engenders two new ones; so that the next generation has a hundred, the next two hundred, the next four hundred, till every human being becomes such a helpless compound of perverted inclina-

[5] Gaster: scilicet Γαστηρ—Venter,—et præterea nihil. [Peacock.] Peacock grew more tolerant of clergymen (Cf. p. 83 ff.); the later ones are gourmets, not gluttons.

tions, that he is altogether at the mercy of external circumstances, loses all independence and singleness of character, and degenerates so rapidly from the primitive dignity of his sylvan origin, that it is scarcely possible to indulge in any other expectation, than that the whole species must at length be exterminated by its own infinite imbecility and vileness.'

'Your opinions,' said Mr. Jenkison, a round-faced little gentleman of about forty-five, 'seem to differ *toto cœlo*. I have often debated the matter in my own mind, *pro* and *con*, and have at length arrived at this conclusion,—that there is not in the human race a tendency either to moral perfectibility or deterioration; but that the quantities of each are so exactly balanced by their reciprocal results, that the species, with respect to the sum of good and evil, knowledge and ignorance, happiness and misery, remains exactly and perpetually in *statu quo*.'

'Surely,' said Mr. Foster, 'you cannot maintain such a proposition in the face of evidence so luminous. Look at the progress of all the arts and sciences,—see chemistry, botany, astronomy——.'

'Surely,' said Mr. Escot, 'experience deposes against you. Look at the rapid growth of corruption, luxury, selfishness ——.'

'Really, gentlemen,' said the Reverend Doctor Gaster, after clearing the husk in his throat with two or three hems, 'this is a very sceptical, and, I must say, atheistical conversation, and I should have thought, out of respect to my cloth——.'

Here the coach stopped, and the coachman, opening the door, vociferated—'Breakfast, gentlemen;' a sound which so gladdened the ears of the divine, that the alacrity with which he sprang from the vehicle superinduced a distortion of his ancle, and he was obliged to limp into the inn between Mr. Escot and Mr. Jenkison; the former observing, that he ought to look for nothing but evil, and, therefore, should not be surprised at this little accident; the latter remarking, that the comfort of a good breakfast, and the pain of a sprained ancle, pretty exactly balanced each other.

*Headlong Hall*, ch. I

Had Fielding or Dickens described those four 'insides' travelling in the Holyhead Mail, the scene would have been quite different. Fielding, if the coach scene in *Joseph Andrews* is indicative, might have had Foster, the 'perfectibilian', robbed of money and clothing, attempting to beg a ride from an acrimonious pessimist and an arrogant and self-seeking clergyman. His caricatures would have been social types who lived as they spoke, whereas Peacock's are representatives of intellectual crotchets—and mere theorists. Instead of tumbling Foster on the roadside, Peacock sets him comfortably beside the other travellers. He creates neither danger nor discomfort.

If he would have offered more action, Fielding would also have begun by introducing himself, as narrator, along with the persons and place. Peacock fills in his scene with a few brief lines. Rather than describe the December morning—as either Fielding or Dickens surely would have done—he merely calls its light 'ambiguous' and forgets it. The characters speak for themselves.

Dickens would have packed his scene (as the coach episodes in *Pickwick* would suggest) with diverse people; their names would have been more obviously humorous, their actions more pronounced, their appearances more detailed. In Dickens, as in Fielding, the narrator would have made his presence, if not his role, more obvious, and he might have made his verbal irony a little less subtle.

Within two pages, Peacock's narrator jumps ahead and reaches behind, in order to give the reader the larger setting, Headlong Hall, and a brief statement about its 'present representative'. His method here is reminiscent of Johnson's *Rasselas*. He establishes *Headlong Hall* itself in the Welsh mountains, an area almost as secluded as Johnson's 'happy valley'; in *Crotchet Castle*, Peacock describes the house as lying in one of those 'pleasant valleys' along the Thames, and there he actually echoes Johnson's story. Ironically, both the houses of Crotchet and Headlong—as the names reveal—begin as idle, and rather foolish, retreats; but they change as the stories progress. Peacock uses them, in other words, much as Johnson had used his hidden valley, first as a burlesquing mirror of the world, and later as a necessary alternative to it.

Peacock's titles are usually meant to be humorous, and all but two—the 'romances'—take their name from the principal stage of the novel. In one sense, his houses are simply stationary coaches: small and restricted places where people talk rather than act. Little changes when the four 'insides' change their podium and arrive at Squire Headlong's estate.

Peacock's settings are intellectual vanity fairs, but limited ones, too. Thackeray took himself off to France and Belgium, and he moved around England at will, in *Vanity Fair*. The scope and the size of his book maybe demanded the geographic and temporal range, and the title itself suggests a sweeping picture rather than a tight, coherent story. Peacock's novels always include some travel, but it is an entire group, *the* group, that travels. The hall or castle, or at least its culinary amenities, seems to move with them. His novels are not only restricted in space, they also occupy little time. With *Maid Marian* and *The Misfortunes of Elphin* partially excepted, Peacock's stories may be said to include the time necessary for a short courtship. Of history, biography, of sub-plots, and long descriptions, the narrator has little to offer. He introduces his people, gives them a pleasant stage, and lets them talk. In his conclusion, however, Peacock comes closer to Fielding and Dickens than he does to Johnson. When the various lovers have surmounted their (usually trivial) difficulties, the curtain drops on anticipated happiness.

# *His people and their talk*

In 'An Essay on Comedy', George Meredith spoke about the necessity for leisure, which would assure comic characters the opportunity for witty talk. His theory of comedy is debatable, and it probably excludes too much, but it does work as a description of Peacock's stories (which, influenced Meredith's own). As any chapter of any of his novels will show, Peacock's characters are isolated and independent of worldly cares. No one has to worry about feeding himself or his family; almost no one participates in the world of commerce. To a certain extent Professor Mario Praz (in *The Hero in Eclipse in Victorian Fiction*) is right when he calls Peacock 'middle class in every paragraph'. While an occasional aristocrat enters into Peacock's world, almost no paupers or workers do. His people are wealthy middle class—at least in their economic position. But they are also people with little class consciousness. Mr. Praz could not be more wrong when he describes their—and their author's—attitudes in terms of prevailing middle-class opinions.

Money is assured in Peacock's stories, or rather it is assumed. Like some of Dickens's, his people may live off the fat of the bourgeois economy even as they speak against its evils; but the important point is that they do speak against mindless consuming and hypocritical stuffiness. Their talk is representative, not of mill owners, but of intellectuals, though Peacock, in Meredith's sense, insures comedy by giving them the wealth of mill owners. Probably no other nineteenth-century English fiction offers a more scathing and consistent attack on the smugness and the cant of the times.

Peacock's novels, nevertheless, hardly seem reformative; he wrote no *Sybil* or *Bleak House*. In *Melincourt*, prompted perhaps by Shelley, he did indict most social and political trends of his time, but the indictment reads like a letter from far away. The finger points, the accusations are made, without however being insisted upon and—more important—without much altering the lives of the characters. Even in *Melincourt*, where the group wanders from one social blight to another, none of the central characters is much affected by the exposed suffering.

Peacock's kind of satire is naturally related to the kind of characters he preferred to draw. While *Gryll Grange* indicates that he could sketch a developing and complex person, the remainder of his stories show that his interest lay elsewhere. He preferred caricature or, to use his own phrase, 'embodied classifications'. Suffering is beyond them as it is irrelevant to Peacock's type of novel. If a reader is to sympathise with any of Peacock's characters, he does so rather because they take part in comic rituals than that they invite any personal involvement.

*Nightmare Abbey* parodies many aspects of German and English romanticism, from the sentiment and plot of Goethe's *Sorrows of Young Werther* to the humanitarian escapades of Shelley's intellectual puberty. Whereas *Melin-*

*court* had focused on social and political ills, *Nightmare Abbey* laughs at artificial *weltschmertz* and other pronounced symptoms of what Peacock considered unhealthy tendencies of the mind. In this book he mocks whining poetasters, intellectual 'specialists', and various other representatives of early nineteenth-century literature.

The portrait of Scythrop (whose name means 'lowering brow') is based upon Shelley; Peacock satirises his pamphleteering, his utopianism, even his vacillation with women. But Scythrop is both more and less than the real Shelley. He embodies characteristics—laughable characteristics—that Shelley did not have, and he represents qualities that, by 1818, Shelley had outgrown. Shelley himself was delighted by the portrait. In the same way, Mr. Flosky is based upon Coleridge, or rather upon Coleridge's reputation, for Peacock was more interested in the ideas than in the man himself. Byron appears as Mr. Cypress, but Cypress parodies only Byron's mawkish side (in fact he speaks pastiches from Byron's silliest poems). Other characters may also be identified: Mr. Toobad caricatures J. F. Newton, a vegetarian and a 'zodiacal mythologist'; Mr. Listless is based upon a boyhood friend of Shelley. But if Peacock's models were—and remain—recognisable, the characters based upon them have an independent fictional life. Peacock's novels are not simply *romans a clefs* in which fictional characters serve as faintly disguised but recognisable living men. As witty spokesmen and types, meeting in their own world, his characters are something more than keys to outside lives.

Byron, after reading *Nightmare Abbey*, asked that Shelley forward a rosebud to Peacock, perhaps to show his appreciation of the poem *Rhododaphne* (Daphne of the rose) as well as *Nightmare Abbey*. Byron knew of course that satire, like a book review, does not kill. Whatever killed John Keats, for example, it was not the *Quarterly*, 'so savage and Tartarly'. But Byron also knew that attacks could hurt; hence his later regret at the acidity of *English Bards and Scotch Reviewers*. His rosebud to Peacock might be understood as his recognition of the genial tone of Peacock's burlesque—and his laughing applause of it.

## 4

## *'The Toast'*

Scythrop, attending one day the summons to dinner, found in the drawing-room his friend Mr. Cypress the poet, whom he had known at college, and who was a great favourite of Mr. Glowry. Mr. Cypress said, he was on the point of leaving England, but could not think of doing so without a farewell-look at Nightmare Abbey and his respected friends, the moody Mr. Glowry and the mysterious Mr. Scythrop, the sublime Mr. Flosky and the pathetic Mr. Listless; to all of whom, and the morbid hospitality of the melancholy dwelling in which they were then assembled, he assured them he should always look back with as much affection as his lacerated spirit could feel for any thing. The sympathetic condolence of their respective replies was cut short by Raven's announcement of 'dinner on table'.

The conversation that took place when the wine was in circulation, and the ladies were withdrawn, we shall report with our usual scrupulous fidelity.

MR. GLOWRY

You are leaving England, Mr. Cypress. There is a delightful melancholy in saying farewell to an old acquaintance, when the chances are twenty to one against ever meeting again. A smiling bumper to a sad parting, and let us all be unhappy together.

MR. CYPRESS (*filling a bumper*)

This is the only social habit that the disappointed spirit never unlearns.

THE REVEREND MR. LARYNX (*filling*)

It is the only piece of academical learning that the finished educatee retains.

MR. FLOSKY (*filling*)

It is the only objective fact which the sceptic can realise.

SCYTHROP (*filling*)

It is the only styptic for a bleeding heart.

THE HONOURABLE MR. LISTLESS (*filling*)

It is the only trouble that is very well worth taking

MR. ASTERIAS (*filling*)

It is the only key of conversational truth.

MR. TOOBAD (*filling*)

It is the only antidote to the great wrath of the devil.

MR. HILARY (*filling*)

It is the only symbol of perfect life. The inscription 'HIC NON BIBITUR' will suit nothing but a tombstone.

MR. GLOWRY

You will see many fine old ruins, Mr. Cypress; crumbling pillars, and mossy walls—many a one-legged Venus and headless Minerva—many a Neptune buried in sand—many a Jupiter turned topsy-turvy—many a perforated Bacchus doing duty as a water-pipe—many reminiscences of the ancient world, which I hope was better worth living in than the modern; though, for myself, I care not a straw more for one than the other, and would not go twenty miles to see any thing that either could show.

MR. CYPRESS

It is something to seek, Mr. Glowry. The mind is restless, and must persist in seeking, though to find is to be disappointed. Do you feel no aspirations towards the countries of Socrates and Cicero? No wish to wander among the venerable remains of the greatness that has passed for ever?

MR. GLOWRY

Not a grain.

SCYTHROP

It is, indeed, much the same as if a lover should dig up the buried form of his mistress, and gaze upon relics which are any thing but herself, to wander among a few mouldy ruins, that are only imperfect indexes to lost volumes of glory, and meet at every step the more melancholy ruins of human nature—a degenerate race of stupid and shrivelled slaves, grovelling in the lowest depths of servility and superstition.

THE HONOURABLE MR. LISTLESS

It is the fashion to go abroad. I have thought of it myself, but am hardly equal to the exertion. To be sure, a little eccentricity and originality are allowable in some cases; and the most eccentric and original of all characters is an Englishman who stays at home.

SCYTHROP

I should have no pleasure in visiting countries that are past all hope of regeneration. There is great hope of our own; and it seems to me that an Englishman, who, either by his station in society, or by his genius, or (as in your instance, Mr. Cypress,) by both, has the power of essentially serving his country in its arduous struggle with its domestic enemies, yet forsakes his country, which is still so rich in hope, to dwell in others which are only fertile in the ruins of memory, does what none of those ancients, whose fragmentary memorials you venerate, would have done in similar circumstances.

MR. CYPRESS

Sir, I have quarrelled with my wife; and a man who has quarrelled with his wife is absolved from all duty to his country. I have written an ode to tell the people as much, and they may take it as they list.

SCYTHROP

Do you suppose, if Brutus had quarrelled with his wife, he would have given it as a reason to Cassius for having nothing to do with his enterprise? Or would Cassius have been satisfied with such an excuse?

MR. FLOSKY

Brutus was a senator; so is our dear friend: but the cases are different. Brutus had some hope of political good: Mr. Cypress has none. How should he, after what we have seen in France?

SCYTHROP

A Frenchman is born in harness, ready saddled, bitted, and bridled, for any tyrant to ride. He will fawn under his rider one moment, and throw him and kick him to death the next; but another adventurer springs on his back, and by dint of whip and spur on he goes as before. We may, without much vanity, hope better of ourselves.

MR. CYPRESS

I have no hope for myself or for others. Our life is a false nature; it is not in the harmony of things; it is an all-blasting upas, whose root is earth, and whose leaves are the skies which rain their poison-dews upon mankind.

We wither from our youth; we gasp with unslaked thirst for unattainable good; lured from the first to the last by phantoms—love, fame, ambition, avarice—all idle, and all ill—one meteor of many names that vanishes in the smoke of death.[6]

MR. FLOSKY

A most delightful speech, Mr. Cypress. A most amiable and instructive philosophy. You have only to impress its truth on the minds of all living men, and life will then, indeed, be the desert and the solitude; and I must do you, myself, and our mutual friends, the justice to observe, that let society only give fair play at one and the same time, as I flatter myself it is inclined to do, to your system of morals, and my system of metaphysics, and Scythrop's system of politics, and Mr. Listless's system of manners, and Mr. Toobad's system of religion, and the result will be as fine a mental chaos as even the immortal Kant himself could ever have hoped to see; in the prospect of which I rejoice.

MR. HILARY

'Certainly, ancient, it is not a thing to rejoice at:' I am one of those who cannot see the good that is to result from all this mystifying and blue-devilling of society. The contrast it presents to the cheerful and solid wisdom of antiquity is too forcible not to strike any one who has the least knowledge of classical literature. To represent vice and misery as the necessary accompaniments of genius, is as mischievous as it is false, and the feeling is as unclassical as the language in which it is usually expressed.

MR. TOOBAD

It is our calamity. The devil has come among us, and has begun by taking possession of all the cleverest fellows.

[6] *Childe Harold*, canto 4. cxxiv. cxxvi. [Peacock.]

Yet, forsooth, this is the enlightened age. Marry, how? Did our ancestors go peeping about with dark lanterns, and do we walk at our ease in broad sunshine? Where is the manifestation of our light? By what symptoms do you recognise it? What are its signs, its tokens, its symptoms, its symbols, its categories, its conditions? What is it, and why? How, where, when is it to be seen, felt, and understood? What do we see by it which our ancestors saw not, and which at the same time is worth seeing? We see a hundred men hanged, where they saw one. We see five hundred transported, where they saw one. We see five thousand in the workhouse, where they saw one. We see scores of Bible Societies, where they saw none. We see paper, where they saw gold. We see men in stays, where they saw men in armour. We see painted faces, where they saw healthy ones. We see children perishing in manufactories, where they saw them flourishing in the fields. We see prisons, where they saw castles. We see masters, where they saw representatives. In short they saw true men, where we see false knaves. They saw Milton, and we see Mr. Sackbut.[7]

MR. FLOSKY

The false knave, sir, is my honest friend; therefore, I beseech you, let him be countenanced. God forbid but a knave should have some countenance at his friend's request.

MR. TOOBAD

'Good men and true' was their common term, like the *καλος κἀγαθος* of the Athenians. It is so long since men have been either good or true, that it is to be questioned which is most obsolete, the fact or the phraseology.

MR. CYPRESS

There is no worth nor beauty but in the mind's idea.

[7] i.e., Robert Southey.

Love sows the wind and reaps the whirlwind.[8] Confusion, thrice confounded, is the portion of him who rests even for an instant on that most brittle of reeds—the affection of a human being. The sum of our social destiny is to inflict or to endure.[9]

MR. HILARY

Rather to bear and forbear, Mr. Cypress—a maxim which you perhaps despise. Ideal beauty is not the mind's creation: it is real beauty, refined and purified in the mind's alembic, from the alloy which always more or less accompanies it in our mixed and imperfect nature. But still the gold exists in a very ample degree.

*Nightmare Abbey*, ch. XI

Names are important to Mr. Glowry, that rather hedonistic, would-be melancholic. He has looked long and hard to find servants with sufficiently dark-sounding names. His butler is Raven. His steward is Crow. A sometime footman was Diggory Deathshead, who proved, unfortunately for Glowry, something of a happy-go-lucky rake, and who had, by the time he was given his papers, left 'a flourishing colony of young Deathsheads' behind him. Peacock makes Glowry a victim of names, and he shares with the reader this time-honoured source of humour.

Of the guests that descend upon Nightmare Abbey, most have qualities identified by their names. Mr. Toobad is of course a confirmed pessimist; Mr. Hilary is happy and genial; and Mr. Listless is listless. Names, then, are as important to Peacock as they are to Mr. Glowry, and he uses them consistently as a badge for caricatures. Some are simply names of qualities; some are puns on Greek or Latin

[8] *Childe Harold*, canto 4. cxxiii. [Peacock.]

[9] *Ibid.* canto 3. lxxi. [Peacock.]

names; some, like those of Dickens, are mere nonsense names.

Peacock follows in a long tradition when he uses names with recognisable meanings. Toobad might be from Bunyan, Listless from Fielding. The difference is that, unlike Bunyan's, for example, Peacock's characters have other qualities; that is, they talk rather than act and do not live according to their ideas. Unlike Fielding's, his characters never become 'life-size'. Again, Peacock creates people of his own first class of comic fiction: embodied characteristics or classifications; because he lets them talk, and because the talk ranges so freely, his people do not remain as mere allegorical figures—despite their names and their protestations.

Yet if they become something more than allegorical figures, they also remain something less than caricatures. Peacock's characters are perhaps best thought of, not as people at all, but as voices. Acting in one way and talking, often simultaneously, in another, they emerge, not so much as embodied classifications, but as disembodied talkers. Oddly enough, few of Peacock's voices are recognisable—as many of Dickens's are—by syntax or conversational tone. They have their favourite words, and they repeat themselves but they are no more complex in their talk than they are in their personalities. One might expect the pace of his novels to suffer, but usually it does not. Peacock rarely lets any voice spout for more than the length of a good-sized paragraph. Then comes an interruption: a round of bottles, a call to dinner, a request for a song—or a physical upset. His conversations are at once endless and regularly brought to an end.

Peacock does make differences among his voices, if not in a conventional novelistic way. He keeps some of his people mere recorders of a caricatured idea. Mr. Toobad of

*Nightmare Abbey*, for example, repeats one sentence many times within the course of the novel, the humour resulting from the shift in context and the surprise reappearance. This is a device Peacock may have learned from Plautus or Terence. He also creates some people who change within the course of the story, either in the range of their expression, or in their overall role. But there are two even more important character divisions common to all of the stories. In each, beginning with *Headlong Hall*, Peacock creates a group within the larger group. He lets the narrator grow fond of some of the characters, and it is these characters who control most of the talk—and who carry off the women.

Peacock's have been called the most attractive women in nineteenth-century fiction. At least they are rarely drab, shrewish, or silly. Nor are they, like their male counterparts, representatives of intellectual crotchets (with one or two trifling exceptions). They are a peculiar breed nevertheless. Peacock occasionally satirises a greedy matchmaker or a fickle girl, but he prefers to introduce women as an antidote to the fopperies of men. In this, as in the matter of leisure, he might have been Meredith's model for good comedy. Meredith suggested that the battle of the sexes, as waged in Molière and in Restoration Comedy, offered the best format for comedy. Peacock sometimes, as in *Crotchet Castle*, matches a lady against her lover in a battle of words; Lady Clarinda, for example, is reminiscent of Congreve's Millamant. His more common device is to keep the women right by keeping them out of entangling conversation. They will either soothe discord by singing and reciting (and all are musically inclined as well as young and beautiful), or they will remain tacit exponents of good sense. When the verbal or amorous battles are at last resolved, they marry their lovers and help to bring about the comic resolution. As a feminist, Peacock seems to have weighed the intelligence of both sexes and found the male wanting, but he is true enough to the conventions of comedy to create high-spirited women who are willing to marry men of questionable mental powers. Lady Clarinda first demolishes Captain Fitzchrome in conversation, then admits her love and marries him. *Nightmare Abbey* concludes rather differently from Peacock's other stories, in that the ladies (Scythrop courts two of them) run off and marry other men. This is probably due to the fact that the plot itself is parody, in part of Goethe's *Werther*, in which the soulful lover takes his own life after a maudlin series of disappointments. Scythrop threatens suicide, but his final gesture is a hearty call for Madeira.

There are few older women in Peacock's fiction, and fewer mothers. A father or a rich uncle serves as guardian of the girl (invariably of marriageable age) and plays a faintly pandaric role in getting her wed. The young men are also motherless. The first chapter of *Nightmare Abbey* is untypical only in that the narrator says something about the death of Mrs. Glowry—One morning, 'like Sir Leoline in Christabel, "he woke and found his lady dead," and remained a very consolate widower, with one small child'.

## *Peacock's narrative and point of view*

There are only a limited number of ways to tell a story, a fact which helps to explain the current flurry of experimentation in narrative prose and the repeated fear that the novel is a dying form. When Peacock wrote, there had already been great experimentation in the novel, though perhaps less in form than in content and purpose. Peacock could adapt the style of any number of writers, French or English, for his purposes. And he did borrow, as we have indicated, widely and freely. His almost supercilious treatment of characters is akin to Fielding's. His reliance on dialogue is akin to Rousseau's and Rousseau's French and English imitators. The love of picturesque description is close to Scott's. But we need to say rather more precisely just what Peacock's narrative does and does not involve—assuming the variety of influences.

Peacock's is consistently a semi-omniscient narrator, who sometimes moves beyond the immediate present but who prefers and dwells in the present. His irony is not based—as Fielding's, George Eliot's, or Thackeray's is—upon the awareness of time and place. Instead his irony is rather verbal, limited to a specific context. Peacock's narrator is close to the conventional narrator of satiric fiction, in that he is anonymous and reticent. Never in his stories do we find the 'I' so prevalent in Scott, or the garrulous and personable speaker so obvious in Fielding. Nor does Peacock relate the story as one of the participating characters, as a Moll Flanders or David Copperfield. The narrator's limited viewpoint perhaps accounts for the shape of Peacock's chapters, each of which, though small, becomes a complete unit, related to what comes before and after, but at the same time independent. We are always in full view of the stage, where the action is punctuated by the falling curtain. If a unifying thread holds the chapters together, it is generally thin: a continuing conversation or a love story.

Peacock takes little interest in any but unusual action, except for eating, drinking, and dancing. Since his novels are usually fast-moving (not only because they are short), and since he delights in brisk talk and physical upsets, Peacock introduces into his stories certain elements of farce. In *Headlong Hall* this is not surprising, for Peacock adapted the novel, with many additions and deletions, from two earlier and unsuccessful farces. Like Dickens, he loved theatre without being able to write successful plays; and also like Dickens, he incorporated into his fiction many aspects of the drama. Farce plays a larger role in *Headlong Hall* than it does in the later novels, but Peacock never lost his delight in upending ridiculous characters and tumbling them head over heels.

One of two landscape gardeners that Squire Headlong has invited to his estate is Mr. Marmaduke Milestone (a caricature based upon the then famous Humphrey Repton). Milestone's bias, as his name indicates, is for regularity, and his aversion is for untamed nature. In the following scene Peacock satirises Milestone's tastes and reveals Headlong's impetuosity. Persuaded by Milestone to 'improve' his estate, the squire calls for Madeira and Gunpowder—and the slapstick begins.

## 5

### *'The Tower'*

The squire and Mr. Milestone,[1] as we have already said, had set out immediately after breakfast to examine the capabilities of the scenery. The object that most attracted Mr. Milestone's admiration was a ruined tower on a projecting point of rock, almost totally overgrown with ivy. This ivy, Mr. Milestone observed, required trimming and clearing in various parts: a little pointing and polishing was also necessary for the dilapidated walls: and the whole effect would be materially increased by a plantation of spruce fir, interspersed with cypress and juniper, the present rugged and broken ascent from the land side being first converted into a beautiful slope, which might be easily effected by blowing up a part of the rock with gunpowder, laying on a quantity of fine mould, and covering the whole with an elegant stratum of turf.

Squire Headlong caught with avidity at this suggestion; and, as he had always a store of gunpowder in the house, for the accommodation of himself and his shooting visitors, and for the supply of a small battery of cannon, which he kept for his private amusement, he insisted on commencing operations immediately. Accordingly, he bounded back to the house, and very speedily returned, accompanied by the little butler, and half a dozen servants and labourers, with pickaxes and gunpowder, a hanging stove and a poker, together with a basket of cold meat and two or three bottles of Madeira: for the Squire thought, with many others, that a copious supply of provision is a very necessary ingredient in all rural amusements.

Mr. Milestone superintended the proceedings. The rock

[1] This is not the actual beginning of the chapter.

was excavated, the powder introduced, the apertures strongly blockaded with fragments of stone: a long train was laid to a spot which Mr. Milestone fixed on as sufficiently remote from the possibility of harm: the Squire seized the poker, and, after flourishing it in the air with a degree of dexterity which induced the rest of the party to leave him in solitary possession of an extensive circumference, applied the end of it to the train; and the rapidly communicated ignition ran hissing along the surface of the soil.

At this critical moment, Mr. Cranium and Mr. Panscope appeared at the top of the tower,[2] which, unseeing and unseen, they had ascended on the opposite side to that where the Squire and Mr. Milestone were conducting their operations. Their sudden appearance a little dismayed the Squire, who, however, comforted himself with the reflection, that the tower was perfectly safe, or at least was intended to be so, and that his friends were in no probable danger but of a knock on the head from a flying fragment of stone.

The succession of these thoughts in the mind of the Squire was commensurate in rapidity to the progress of the ignition, which having reached its extremity, the explosion took place, and the shattered rock was hurled into the air in the midst of fire and smoke.

Mr. Milestone had properly calculated the force of the explosion; for the tower remained untouched: but the Squire, in his consolatory reflections, had omitted the consideration of the influence of sudden fear, which had so violent an effect on Mr. Cranium, who was just commencing a speech concerning the very fine prospect from the top of the tower, that, cutting short the thread of his

[2] Mr. Panscope, 'the chemical, botanical, geological, astronomical, mathematical, metaphysical, meteorological, anatomical, physiological, galvanistical, musical, pictorial, bibliographical, critical philosopher' is another portrait of Coleridge. Mr. Cranium is a caricature of phrenologists, whose 'science' was then in vogue.

observations, he bounded, under the elastic influence of terror, several feet into the air. His ascent being unluckily a little out of the perpendicular, he descended with a proportionate curve from the apex of his projection, and alighted, not on the wall of the tower, but in an ivy-bush by its side, which, giving way beneath him, transferred him to a tuft of hazel at its base, which, after upholding him an instant, consigned him to the boughs of an ash that had rooted itself in a fissure about half way down the rock, which finally transmitted him to the waters below.

Squire Headlong anxiously watched the tower as the smoke which at first enveloped it rolled away; but when this shadowy curtain was withdrawn, and Mr. Panscope was discovered, *solus*, in a tragical attitude, his apprehensions became boundless, and he concluded that the unlucky collision of a flying fragment of rock had indeed emancipated the spirit of the craniologist from its terrestrial bondage.

Mr. Escot had considerably outstripped his companions, and arrived at the scene of the disaster just as Mr. Cranium, being utterly destitute of natatorial skill, was in imminent danger of final submersion. The deteriorationist, who had cultivated this valuable art with great success, immediately plunged in to his assistance, and brought him alive and in safety to a shelving part of the shore. Their landing was hailed with a view-holla from the delighted Squire, who, shaking them both heartily by the hand, and making ten thousand lame apologies to Mr. Cranium, concluded by asking, in a pathetic tone, *How much water he had swallowed?* and without waiting for his answer, filled a large tumbler with Madeira, and insisted on his tossing it off, which was no sooner said than done. Mr. Jenkison and Mr. Foster now made their appearance. Mr. Panscope descended the tower, which he vowed never again to approach within a quarter of a mile. The tumbler of Madeira was replenished, and handed round to recruit the spirits of the party, which now began to move towards Headlong Hall, the Squire capering for joy in the van, and the little fat butler waddling in the rear.

The Squire took care that Mr. Cranium should be seated next to him at dinner, and plied him so hard with Madeira to prevent him, as he said, from taking cold, that long before the ladies sent in their summons to coffee, every organ in his brain was in a complete state of revolution, and the Squire was under the necessity of ringing for three or four servants to carry him to bed, observing, with a smile of great satisfaction, that he was in a very excellent way for escaping any ill consequences that might have resulted from his accident.

The beautiful Cephalis, being thus freed from his *surveillance*, was enabled, during the course of the evening, to develope to his preserver the full extent of her gratitude.

*Headlong Hall*, ch. VIII

Peacock's narrator is, quite clearly, an ironist. There is in his manner a discrepancy between the offered and intended; there is always the distorting mirror of burlesque. Squire Headlong, for example, 'commences operations'—like a military strategist—then 'bounds' back to the house—like a kangaroo. Peacock laughs at the improving project by an implied high comparison, and he laughs at Squire Headlong (and his absurd movements) by an apt low comparison. Burlesque works in this way throughout Peacock's stories.

Related to burlesque and to the two incidents mentioned is the matter of diction. Peacock's narrator identifies himself by his peculiar vocabulary, and his vocabulary involves a critical problem. Peacock's serious poems—like Byron's—suffer from imprecise, if not vague, and at the same time hackneyed, diction. Peacock could write poetry that avoided large, opaque phrasings, and he did so increasingly after he gave up writing long and formal poems. He could also write unembellished expository prose, as his Memoirs of Shelley will illustrate. But again like Byron, he loved the big word and the inflated phrase. Mr. Cranium's indecorous fall is told in great detail—from ivy bush to hazel, and so on into the lake. Its quality, however, comes from the mixed vocabulary and the peculiar phrasing as much as from the list of stages. Peacock often indicates speed by increasing the length of his words and, ironically, by insisting on leisurely syntax. The result is slow-moving animation, which serves to burlesque the action.

Peacock's novels all mock pomposity and pedantry, but there is more than a touch of both in the narrator himself. It is well to distinguish between author and narrator, the more so in an author who invites a simple confusion of the two. Following writers like John Bunyan and, closer to his own time, Richard Graves and Samuel Johnson, Peacock prefers to let the characters speak, and his narrator, like his talkative characters, may be thought of as one of his voices, one of his many viewpoints. It is often as though Peacock attaches a narrative framework to an essentially dramatic sequence, as though his narrator serves the real function of imposing order on disorderly talk.

But there are many times when Peacock lets the unidentified narrator (the hovering 'we') spout about the other characters. At these times his characters become closer to those of Fielding—objects of laughter, puppet-like, who are introduced in a laughing and off-hand manner. The narrator in these instances delights in moments of discord or imbalance, and he ends a scene with a restorative drink or song, or, as in the case of Mr. Cranium, with a fall. Because he has created talking dolls, whose responses are predictable, Peacock exploits the anticipation of a rumpus. Given a confirmed landscape gardener and an impetuous squire, we simply wait to see *how* the explosion takes place and with what farcical results.

In short, Peacock borrows from Fielding and Fielding's literary offspring the delight in patronising his characters. As ironist, his narrator partly laughs with the reader at the character's expense. But one essential difference remains, and it is the real line of division between Fielding's type of novel (or Scott's, or Thackeray's) and Peacock's. Peacock's narrator never becomes much of a character himself. He is in fact limited as the other characters are limited —to a kind of caricature. He may be a *poseur,* but he pretends rather to record than to know.

# *Comedy*

Peacock's is sophisticated comedy, an exuberant game of words, a running exchange of wit and opinion, as allusionary as it is fast moving. At first glance a reader would be unlikely to associate Peacock's books with ancient comedy or, to go even farther back, with the assumed origins of comedy in ritual and dance. He would be more apt to compare Peacock with Congreve or Molière than with the Dionysian rites or with the historical outgrowth of those rites in a writer like Aristophanes. In fact, most of Peacock's readers have devoted their energies to the divining of what he intended, whom he lampooned, on which heads his satiric sword landed; they have discussed his comedy in terms of satiric intent rather than literary qualities. Much can be said about his satire (and something will be said in the following section) but much can also be said about his comedy, comedy thought of as a ritualistic art form, in which satire plays only one of several parts.

Despite the range of types and subjects and the varieties of comic poets, the basic attributes of comedy are few. Mr. Wiley Sypher (in his introduction to Meredith's 'An

Essay on Comedy' and Henri Bergson's 'Laughter') speaks of them as the Ritual and the Dance, the Feast and the Sacrifice, his implication being that all comedy re-enacts the traditions of the old festivals. In Peacock's novels these features of comedy are especially obvious. It is a combination of overt comic ritual and witty dialectic that gives his comedy its distinctive qualities. For his material was the intellectual aberrations of his times, which he imposed upon a comic tradition as old as Aristophanes.

In his last novel, *Gryll Grange*, Peacock presents what he entitles an 'Aristophanic Comedy'. He calls forth the spirit of Aristophanes and of other ancients and bids them comment—they do so with alacrity—on the lamentable conditions of modern England. The Comedy becomes a relevant part of *Gryll Grange*, since it involves preparations, experiments in staging, talking, and writing, all of which occupy the characters for a few weeks. Yet the kind of comedy that Aristophanes supposedly evokes is ironically less important to *Gryll Grange* than to the earlier novels. The final novel contains satire upon the times, some of it damning, but the satire is expressed by the entire group of characters, who are not themselves the objects of satire in any major way. Peacock's earlier practice had been to put together a group of quasi-rational creatures, all of them specialists in one absurd field or another, in order to let them prove that none was worth his salt as a thinker. Like Socrates and his cohorts in *The Clouds*, they lose themselves in etherised ideas. Consider what happens in *Crotchet Castle*. Peacock assembles in the castle his most varied group of caricatures. They talk, they almost fight, they agree on nothing. In the battle of wits some are made victims: Mr. Henbane, an experimentor in poisons, dies by his own medicine; Mr. Eavesdrop, a noted gossip, loses his social credentials. They become, in other words, the scapegoats, the *alazons* or victims, of comedy. They are purged of folly by an overdose of folly. While they are being sacrificed (perhaps to common sense), the other characters are mollified by the beneficent attributes of Port and Madeira and by the soothing qualities of a well-appointed table. Mr. Chainmail (a medievalist) lifts an ancient goblet in constant toast, and the Reverend Doctor Folliott (a hedonist) praises lobster at breakfast. The action of the story begins at a breakfast and closes with an elaborate dinner.

Peacock insists on the ritual and the dance, which are almost inseperable, as much as on the sacrifice and the feast. He usually introduces dances in his stories, but *dance* conceived of as the overall movement of characters to music, involves more than a simple evening ball. Later in the nineteenth century Friedrich Nietzsche was to speak about the Dionysian qualities of music and to equate music with ancient festivals and with the power underlying both tragedy and comedy. Peacock hints in some of his music criticism at a similar idea, and his appreciation of modern opera was based, he said, on its affinity with Athenian drama. In his novels music plays an important part. The heroines sing and thereby restore order; and the songs comment on and extend the narrative. Dance and music are also associated with festival. *Headlong Hall*, the first novel, begins appropriately in December, when guests of the squire are arriving at the hall to celebrate the winter holiday. The novel ends, not only with the ritual holidays, but with the ritual weddings of the comic characters, with what Peacock calls 'the spiritual metamorphosis of eight into four'. Peacock shared with several writers of his age—Hazlitt, Leigh Hunt, and Charles Lamb among them—the fear that such festivals as May Day would die out. As an old man he sponsored celebrations in the country around his house. His novels, like those of Dickens, offer paeans to the delights of eating, drinking, and companionship—in other words to festive rituals—and Peacock, like Dickens, educates his Scrooges in those delights.

Peacock once wrote that the only bright spot in the middle ages was the kitchen fire; the comment both reinforces the fact of his culinary interests and characterises his estimate of the times. He shared the common, and largely ill-founded, notion of the 'dark ages', in which he imagined round-bellied monks and blustering barons wandering in ignorance through greensward. *Maid Marian*, dealing with Robin Hood, Marian, Little John, and the rest, reveals Peacock as a misinformed and cavalier historian. The book represented a new venture for him. He started to write it shortly after the completion of *Nightmare Abbey*, then abandoned it for three years when he began employment in the India House. He seems not to have been eager to finish it, perhaps realising that satiric romance was not his strength, and that brilliant passages could not carry an entire book.

Though short, much of *Maid Marian* is tedious. It is not one of his best stories. Since Peacock's talk is better than his narrative, the reason for the book's failure may lie here. Yet however much Peacock might have been out of his element in *Maid Marian*, however weak may have been the conception, some half dozen sections are among his best. In the following passage, which occurs before Matilda—soon to be Marian—leaves for Sherwood and the friar becomes the redoubtable Friar Tuck, Peacock lets them indulge in a Rabelaisian exchange with Matilda's father. Here, as in much of the story, dialogue gives way to song.

## 6

## *'Maid Marian'*

> Are you mad, or what are you, that you squeak out your coziers' catches without mitigation or remorse of voice?
>
> *Twelfth Night*

Matilda, not dreaming of visitors, tripped into the apartment in a dress of forest green, with a small quiver by her side, and a bow and arrow in her hand. Her hair, black and glossy as the raven's wing, curled like wandering clusters of dark ripe grapes under the edge of her round bonnet; and a plume of black feathers fell back negligently above it, with an almost horizontal inclination, that seemed the habitual effect of rapid motion against the wind. Her black eyes sparkled like sunbeams on a river: a clear, deep, liquid radiance, the reflection of ethereal fire,—tempered, not subdued, in the medium of its living and gentle mirror. Her lips were half opened to speak as she entered the apartment; and with a smile of recognition to the friar, and a courtesy to the stranger knight, she approached the baron and said, 'You are late at your breakfast, father.'

'I am not at breakfast,' said the baron. 'I have been at supper: my last night's supper; for I had none.'

'I am sorry,' said Matilda, 'you should have gone to bed supperless.'

'I did not go to bed supperless,' said the baron: 'I did not go to bed at all: and what are you doing with that green dress and that bow and arrow?'

'I am going a-hunting,' said Matilda.

'A-hunting!' said the baron. 'What, I warrant you, to meet with the earl, and slip your neck into the same noose?'

'No,' said Matilda: 'I am not going out of our own woods to-day.'

'How do I know that?' said the baron. 'What surety have I of that?'

'Here is the friar,' said Matilda. 'He will be surety.'

'Not he,' said the baron: 'he will undertake nothing but where the devil is a party concerned.'

'Yes, I will,' said the friar: 'I will undertake any thing for the lady Matilda.'

'No matter for that,' said the baron: 'she shall not go hunting to-day.'

'Why, father,' said Matilda, 'if you coop me up here in this odious castle, I shall pine and die like a lonely swan on a pool.'

'No,' said the baron, 'the lonely swan does not die on the pool. If there be a river at hand, she flies to the river, and finds her a mate; and so shall not you.'

'But,' said Matilda, 'you may send with me any, or as many, of your grooms as you will.'

'My grooms,' said the baron, 'are all false knaves. There is not a rascal among them but loves you better than me. Villains that I feed and clothe.'

'Surely,' said Matilda, 'it is not villany to love me: if it be, I should be sorry my father were an honest man.' The baron relaxed his muscles into a smile. 'Or my lover either,' added Matilda. The baron looked grim again.

'For your lover,' said the baron, 'you may give God thanks of him. He is as arrant a knave as ever poached.'

'What, for hunting the king's deer?' said Matilda. 'Have I not heard you rail at the forest laws by the hour?'

'Did you ever hear me,' said the baron, 'rail myself out of house and land? If I had done that, then were I a knave.'

'My lover,' said Matilda, 'is a brave man, and a true man, and a generous man, and a young man, and a handsome man; aye, and an honest man too.'

'How can he be an honest man,' said the baron, 'when he has neither house nor land, which are the better part of a man?'

'They are but the husk of a man,' said Matilda, 'the worthless coat of the chesnut: the man himself is the kernel.'

'The man is the grape stone,' said the baron, 'and the pulp of the melon. The house and land are the true substantial fruit, and all that give him savour and value.'

'He will never want house or land,' said Matilda, 'while the meeting boughs weave a green roof in the wood, and the free range of the hart marks out the bounds of the forest.'

'Vert and venison! vert and venison!' exclaimed the baron. 'Treason and flat rebellion. Confound your smiling face! what makes you look so good-humoured? What! you think I can't look at you, and be in a passion? You think so, do you? We shall see. Have you no fear in talking thus, when here is the king's liegeman come to take us all into custody, and confiscate our goods and chattels?'

'Nay, Lord Fitzwater,' said Sir Ralph, 'you wrong me in your report. My visit is one of courtesy and excuse, not of menace and authority.'

'There it is,' said the baron: 'every one takes a pleasure in contradicting me. Here is this courteous knight, who has not opened his mouth three times since he has been in my house except to take in provision, cuts me short in my story with a flat denial.'

'Oh! I cry you mercy, sir knight,' said Matilda; 'I did not mark you before. I am your debtor for no slight favour, and so is my liege lord.'[1]

'Her liege lord!' exclaimed the baron, taking large strides across the chamber.

'Pardon me, gentle lady,' said Sir Ralph. 'Had I known you before yesterday, I would have cut off my right hand ere it should have been raised to do you displeasure.'

'Oh sir,' said Matilda, 'a good man may be forced on an ill office: but I can distinguish the man from his duty.' She presented to him her hand, which he kissed respectfully, and simultaneously with the contact thirty-two in-

[1] As the king's agent, Sir Ralph has previously interrupted Matilda's wedding with her 'liege lord', Robin Hood.

visible arrows plunged at once into his heart, one from every point of the compass of his pericardia.

'Well, father,' added Matilda, 'I must go to the woods.'

'Must you?' said the baron; 'I say you must not.'

'But I am going,' said Matilda.

'But I will have up the drawbridge,' said the baron.

'But I will swim the moat,' said Matilda.

'But I will secure the gates,' said the baron.

'But I will leap from the battlement,' said Matilda.

'But I will lock you in an upper chamber,' said the baron.

'But I will shred the tapestry,' said Matilda, 'and let myself down.'

'But I will lock you in a turret,' said the baron, 'where you shall only see light through a loophole.'

'But through that loophole,' said Matilda, 'will I take my flight, like a young eagle from its aerie; and, father, while I go out freely, I will return willingly: but if once I slip out through a loophole——' She paused a moment, and then added, singing,—

> The love that follows fain
>    Will never its faith betray:
> But the faith that is held in a chain
> Will never be found again,
>    If a single link give way.

The melody acted irresistibly on the harmonious propensities of the friar, who accordingly sang in his turn,—

> For hark! hark! hark!
> The dog doth bark,
>    That watches the wild deer's lair.
> The hunter awakes at the peep of the dawn,
> But the lair it is empty, the deer it is gone,
>    And the hunter knows not where.

Matilda and the friar then sang together,—

> Then follow, oh follow! the hounds do cry:

The red sun flames in the eastern sky:
  The stag bounds over the hollow.
He that lingers in spirit, or loiters in hall,
Shall see us no more till the evening fall,
And no voice but the echo shall answer his call:
  Then follow, oh follow, follow:
  Follow, oh follow, follow!

During the process of this harmony, the baron's eyes wandered from his daughter to the friar, and from the friar to his daughter again, with an alternate expression of anger differently modified: when he looked on the friar, it was anger without qualification; when he looked on his daughter it was still anger, but tempered by an expression of involuntary admiration and pleasure. These rapid fluctuations of the baron's physiognomy—the habitual, reckless, resolute merriment in the jovial face of the friar,—and the cheerful, elastic spirits that played on the lips and sparkled in the eyes of Matilda,—would have presented a very amusing combination to Sir Ralph, if one of the three images in the group had not absorbed his total attention with feelings of intense delight very nearly allied to pain. The baron's wrath was somewhat counteracted by the reflection that his daughter's good spirits seemed to show that they would naturally rise triumphant over all disappointments; and he had had sufficient experience of her humour to know that she might sometimes be led, but never could be driven. Then, too, he was always delighted to hear her sing, though he was not at all pleased in this instance with the subject of her song. Still he would have endured the subject for the sake of the melody of the treble, but his mind was not sufficiently attuned to unison to relish the harmony of the bass. The friar's accompaniment put him out of all patience, and—'So,' he exclaimed, 'this is the way, you teach my daughter to renounce the devil, is it? A hunting friar, truly! Who ever heard before of a hunting friar? A profane, roaring, bawling, bumper-bibbing, neck-breaking, catch-singing friar?'

'Under favour, bold baron,' said the friar; but the friar was warm with canary, and in his singing vein; and he could not go on in plain unmusical prose. He therefore sang in a new tune,—

Though I be now a grey, grey friar,
  Yet I was once a hale young knight:
The cry of my dogs was the only choir
  In which my spirit did take delight.
Little I recked of matin bell,
  But drowned its toll with my clanging horn:
And the only beads I loved to tell
  Were the beads of dew on the spangled thorn.

The baron was going to storm, but the friar paused, and Matilda sang in repetition,—

Little I reck of matin bell,
  But drown its toll with my clanging horn:
And the only beads I love to tell
  Are the beads of dew on the spangled thorn.

And then she and the friar sang the four lines together, and rang the changes upon them alternately.

Little I reck of matin bell,

sang the friar.

'A precious friar,' said the baron.

But drown its toll with my clanging horn,

sang Matilda.

'More shame for you,' said the baron.

And the only beads I love to tell
  Are the beads of dew on the spangled thorn,

sang Matilda and the friar together.

'Penitent and confessor,' said the baron: 'a hopeful pair truly.'

The friar went on,—

> An archer keen I was withal,
> As ever did lean on greenwood tree;
> And could make the fleetest roebuck fall,
> A good three hundred yards from me.
> Though changeful time, with hand severe,
> Has made me now these joys forego,
> Yet my heart bounds whene'er I hear
> Yoicks! hark away! and tally ho!

Matilda chimed in as before.

'Are you mad?' said the baron. 'Are you insane? Are you possessed? What do you mean? What in the devil's name do you both mean?'

> Yoicks! hark away! and tally ho!

roared the friar.

The baron's pent-up wrath had accumulated like the waters above the dam of an overshot mill. The pond-head of his passion being now filled to the utmost limit of its capacity, and beginning to overflow in the quivering of his lips and the flashing of his eyes, he pulled up all the flash-boards at once, and gave loose to the full torrent of his indignation, by seizing, like furious Ajax, not a massy stone more than two modern men could raise, but a vast dish of beef more than fifty ancient yeomen could eat, and whirled it like a coit, *in terrorem*, over the head of the friar, to the extremity of the apartment,

> Where it on oaken floor did settle,
> With mighty din of ponderous metal.

'Nay father,' said Matilda, taking the baron's hand, 'do not harm the friar: he means not to offend you. My gaiety never before displeased you. Least of all should it do so now, when I have need of all my spirits to outweigh the severity of my fortune.'

As she spoke the last words, tears started into her eyes,

which, as if ashamed of the involuntary betraying of her feelings, she turned away to conceal. The baron was subdued at once. He kissed his daughter, held out his hand to the friar, and said, 'Sing on, in God's name, and crack away the flasks till your voice swims in canary.' Then turning to Sir Ralph, he said, 'You see how it is, sir knight. Matilda is my daughter; but she has me in leading-strings, that is the truth of it.'

*Maid Marian*, ch. IV

*Maid Marian*, as the foregoing scene indicates, is a kind of boisterous romantic comedy. The baron's castle itself represents a 'green' world, which is both rural and 'romantic', where people live in easy retirement (though the baron himself has certain difficulties). But this world will be disturbed by the corrupt outer world of King John's court. Sir Ralph, smitten here by Matilda's charms, is both the king's agent in the search for the Earl of Huntington (Robin Hood) and the first herald of disruption. Even the baron will be forced to leave his castle. As in Shakespeare's *Tempest* and *As You Like It*, the 'good' characters are forced into exile, and they enter the even greener world of Sherwood Forest. Sherwood resembles Shakespeare's forest world, the golden world of Arden, where the Duke and his court fleet away their time. Robin Hood is king here (because 'might equals right' in the burlesque of political institutions), legitimate poacher of the king's deer, legitimate robber of the king's men. He is finally praised for his efforts when King Richard returns to supplant the evil King John. Robin and his crew dine away the time, sing songs—and crack heads. Friar Tuck (still just 'the friar' in the previous scene), who might be a mixture of Gargantua (in stature) and Falstaff (in speech) becomes the irreverent spokesman for worldly pleasures, political rights, and almost everything else. He is the toastmaster in this at once idyllic and absurd romantic world.

Peacock satirises a variety of events and institutions in *Maid Marian*, but none of the characters speak like the monomaniacal types of the novels of talk. If *Maid Marian* is romantic comedy, Peacock's other novels may be thought of as a combination of romantic comedy and comedy of ideas: as though Jacques and Touchstone held court in Shakespeare's Forest of Arden—and married the heroines. The emphasis shifts, however, according to the focus of the novel. *Nightmare Abbey* is largely comedy of humours, because the characters represent kinds of temperament or temperamental affectations as much as intellectual crotchets. When Shelley sent to Peacock a quotation from Ben Jonson's *Every Man in his Humour*, he found it an appropriate motto. One reason for writing the story, he had said, was to shine a little daylight on the morbid fashions of his day, especially the indulgence in sentimental melancholy. With Jonson and many other writers, melancholy had long been a source of 'humour' comedy.

Like the earlier stories, *Gryll Grange* approaches romantic comedy. Characters find a pleasant and secluded retreat at Squire Gryll's estate, far away from cities and cares. But while there is the usual admixture in this novel of romantic retreat, 'ideas', and 'humours', *Gryll Grange* comes much closer than the other novels to comedy of manners. By the time he wrote this novel—he was over seventy—Peacock was as interested in how men lived as in what they thought. The shift is one of emphasis rather than kind, but it is noticeable, and it makes the book rather less accessible to modern readers. Peacock is less Rabelaisian here, less exuberant. The pace of the novel is slower, the novel itself longer, and the tone more subdued.

Some things do remain unchanged. Here, as in the earlier novels, the narrator presents his characters with a topic for conversation, then pretends to stand back and let them talk. The dinner table continued to be Peacock's favourite setting. A gastronome himself, he made his favourite characters into gastronomes too. The opening chapter of *Gryll Grange* offers in miniature the workings of the entire story. Notice how, typically, conversation about food extends into a general discussion about the times.

## 7

### *'Misnomers'*

Ego sic semper et ubique vixi, ut ultimam quamque lucem, tamquam non redituram, consumerem.—PETRONIUS ARBITER.

Always and everywhere I have so lived, that I might consume the passing light, as if it were not to return.

'Palestine soup!' said the Reverend Doctor Opimian, dining with his friend Squire Gryll; 'a curiously complicated misnomer. We have an excellent old vegetable, the artichoke, of which we eat the head; we have another of subsequent introduction, of which we eat the root, and which we also call artichoke, because it resembles the first in flavour, although, *me judice*, a very inferior affair. This last is a species of the helianthus, or sunflower genus of the *Syngenesia frustranea* class of plants. It is therefore a girasol, or turn-to-the-sun. From this girasol we have made Jerusalem, and from the Jerusalem artichoke we make Palestine soup.'

MR. GRYLL

A very good thing, Doctor.

THE REVEREND DOCTOR OPIMIAN

A very good thing; but a palpable misnomer.

MR. GRYLL

I am afraid we live in a world of misnomers, and of a worse kind than this. In my little experience I have found that a gang of swindling bankers is a respectable old firm; that men who sell their votes to the highest bidder, and want only 'the protection of the ballot' to sell the promise of them to both parties, are a free and independent constituency; that a man who successively betrays everybody that trusts him, and abandons every principle he ever professed, is a great statesman, and a Conservative, forsooth, *à nil conservando;* that schemes for breeding pestilence are sanitary improvements; that the test of intellectual capacity is in swallow, and not in digestion; that the art of teaching everything, except what will be of use to the recipient, is national education; and that a change for the worse is reform. Look across the Atlantic.[2] A Sympathizer would seem to imply a certain degree of benevolent feeling. Nothing of the kind. It signifies a ready-made accomplice in any species of political villany. A Know-Nothing[3] would seem to imply a liberal self-diffidence—on the scriptural principle that the beginning of knowledge is to know that thou art ignorant. No such thing. It implies furious political dogmatism, enforced by bludgeons and revolvers. A Locofoco[3] is the only intelligible term: a fellow that would set any place on fire to roast his own eggs. A Filibuster[3] is a pirate under national colours; but I suppose the word in its origin implies something virtuous: perhaps a friend of humanity.

[2] Peacock once thought about immigrating to the New World, probably to Canada, and he had written an appreciative essay on Thomas Jefferson. By the time he wrote *Gryll Grange*, however, he had nothing good to say about America.

[3] These terms were current in American politics of the time.

THE REVEREND DOCTOR OPIMIAN

More likely a friend of roaring—*Φιλοβωστρὴς*—in the sense in which roaring is used by our old dramatists; for which see Middleton's *Roaring Girl,* and the commentators thereon.[4]

MR. GRYLL

While we are on the subject of misnomers, what say you to the wisdom of Parliament?

THE REVEREND DOCTOR OPIMIAN

Why, sir, I do not call that a misnomer. The term wisdom is used in a parliamentary sense. The wisdom of Parliament is a wisdom *sui generis*. It is not like any other wisdom. It is not the wisdom of Socrates, nor the wisdom of Solomon. It is the wisdom of Parliament. It is not easily analysed or defined; but it is very easily understood. It has achieved wonderful things by itself, and still more when Science has come to its aid. Between them, they have poisoned the Thames, and killed the fish in the river. A little further development of the some wisdom and science will complete the poisoning of the air, and kill the dwellers on the banks. It is pleasant that the precious effluvium has been brought so efficiently under the Wisdom's own wise nose. Thereat the nose, like Trinculo's, has been in great indignation. The Wisdom has ordered the Science to do something. The Wisdom does not know what, nor the Science either. But the Wisdom has empowered

[4] '*Roaring boys* was a cant term for the riotous, quarrelsome blades of the time, who abounded in London, and took pleasure in annoying its quieter inhabitants. Of *Roaring Girls,* the heroine of the present play was the choicest specimen. Her real name was *Mary Frith,* but she was most commonly known by that of *Moll Cutpurse.*'—Dyce. She wore male apparel, smoked, fought, robbed on the highway, kept all minor thieves in subjection, and compelled the restitution of stolen goods, when duly paid for her services. [Peacock.]

the Science to spend some millions of money; and this, no doubt, the Science will do. When the money has been spent, it will be found that the something has been worse than nothing. The Science will want more money to do some other something, and the Wisdom will grant it. *Redit labor actus in orbem.*[5] But you have got on moral and political ground. My remark was merely on a perversion of words, of which we have an inexhaustible catalogue.

MR. GRYLL

Whatever ground we take, Doctor, there is one point common to most of these cases: the word presents an idea, which does not belong to the subject, critically considered. Palestine Soup is not more remote from the true Jerusalem, than many an honourable friend from public honesty and honour. However, Doctor, what say you to a glass of old Madeira, which I really believe is what it is called?

THE REVEREND DOCTOR OPIMIAN

*In vino veritas*. I accept with pleasure.

MISS GRYLL

You and my uncle, Doctor, get up a discussion on everything that presents itself; dealing with your theme like a series of variations in music. You have run half round the world *àpropos* of the soup. What say you to the fish?

THE REVEREND DOCTOR OPIMIAN

Premising that this is a remarkably fine slice of salmon, there is much to be said about fish: but not in the way of misnomers. Their names are single and simple. Perch, sole, cod, eel, carp, char, skate, tench, trout, brill, bream, pike,

[5] The labour returns, compelled into a circle. [Peacock.] Quoted from Virgil's *Georgics*.

and many others, plain monosyllables: salmon, dory, turbot, gudgeon, lobster, whitebait, grayling, haddock, mullet, herring, oyster, sturgeon, flounder, turtle, plain dissyllables: only two trisyllables worth naming, anchovy and mackerel; unless any one should be disposed to stand up for halibut, which for my part I have excommunicated.

MR. GRYLL

I agree with you on that point; but I think you have named one or two, that might as well keep it company.

THE REVEREND DOCTOR OPIMIAN

I do not think I have named a single unpresentable fish.

MR. GRYLL

Bream, Doctor: there is not much to be said for bream.

THE REVEREND DOCTOR OPIMIAN

On the contrary, sir, I think there is much to be said for him. In the first place, there is the authority of the monastic brotherhoods, who are universally admitted to have been connoisseurs in fish, and in the mode of preparing it; and you will find bream pie set down as a prominent item of luxurious living in the indictments prepared against them at the dissolution of the monasteries. The work of destruction was rather too rapid, and I fear the receipt is lost. But he can still be served up as an excellent stew, provided always that he is full-grown, and has swum all his life in clear running water. I call everything fish that seas, lakes, and rivers furnish to cookery; though, scientifically, a turtle is a reptile, and a lobster an insect. Fish, Miss Gryll —I could discourse to you on fish by the hour: but for the present I will forbear: as Lord Curryfin is coming down to Thornback Bay, to lecture the fishermen on fish and fisheries, and to astonish them all with the science of their art. You will, no doubt, be curious to hear him. There will be some reserved seats.

MISS GRYLL

I shall be very curious to hear him, indeed. I have never heard a lecturing lord. The fancy of lords and gentlemen to lecture everybody on everything, everywhere, seems to me something very comical; but perhaps it is something very serious, gracious in the lecturer, and instructive to the audience. I shall be glad to be cured of my unbecoming propensity to laugh, whenever I hear of a lecturing lord.

THE REVEREND DOCTOR OPIMIAN

I hope, Miss Gryll, you will not laugh at Lord Curryfin: for you may be assured, nothing will be farther from his lordship's intention than to say anything in the slightest degree droll.

MR. GRYLL

Doctor Johnson was astonished at the mania for lectures, even in his day, when there were no lecturing lords. He thought little was to be learned from lectures, unless where, as in chemistry, the subject required illustration by experiment. Now, if your lord is going to exhibit experiments, in the art of cooking fish, with specimens in sufficient number for all his audience to taste, I have no doubt his lecture will be well attended, and a repetition earnestly desired.

THE REVEREND DOCTOR OPIMIAN

I am afraid the lecture will not have the aid of such pleasant adventitious attractions. It will be a pure scientific exposition, carefully classified, under the several divisions and subdivisions of Ichthyology, Entomology, Herpetology, and Conchology. But I agree with Doctor Johnson, that little is to be learned from lectures. For the most part, those who do not already understand the subject will not understand the lecture, and those who do will learn nothing from it. The latter will hear many things they would like to contradict, which the *bienséance* of the lecture-room does not allow. I do not comprehend how people can find amusement in lectures. I should much prefer a *tenson* of the twelfth century, when two or three masters of the *Gai Saber* discussed questions of love and chivalry.[6]

MISS GRYLL

I am afraid, Doctor, our age is too prosy for that sort of thing. We have neither wit enough, nor poetry enough, to furnish the disputants. I can conceive a state of society in which such *tensons* would form a pleasant winter evening amusement: but that state of society is not ours.

THE REVEREND DOCTOR OPIMIAN

Well, Miss Gryll, I should like, some winter evening, to challenge you to a *tenson*, and your uncle should be umpire. I think you have wit enough by nature, and I have poetry enough by memory, to supply a fair portion of the requisite materials, without assuming an absolute mastery of the *Gai Saber*.

MISS GRYLL

I shall accept the challenge, Doctor. The wit on one side will, I am afraid, be very shortcoming; but the poetry on the other will no doubt be abundant.

MR. GRYLL

Suppose, Doctor, you were to get up a *tenson* a little more relative to our own wise days. Spirit-rapping, for example, is a fine field. *Nec pueri credunt. . . Sed tu vera puta.*[7] You might go beyond the limits of a *tenson*. There is ample scope for an Aristophanic comedy. In the contest between the Just and the Unjust in the *Clouds*, and in other scenes of Aristophanes, you have ancient specimens of

[6] *Tenson*: a kind of verse dialogue or contest. *Gai Saber*: the art or science of poetry.

[7] Not even boys believe it: but suppose it to be true. [Peacock.] Quoted from Juvenal, *Satires*.

something very like *tensons*, except that Love has not much share in them. Let us for a moment suppose this same spirit-rapping to be true—dramatically so, at least. Let us fit up a stage for the purpose: make the invoked spirits visible as well as audible: and calling before us some of the illustrious of former days, ask them what they think of us and our doings? Of our astounding progress of intellect? Our march of mind? Our higher tone of morality? Our vast diffusion of education? Our art of choosing the most unfit man by competitive examination?

THE REVEREND DOCTOR OPIMIAN

You had better not bring on many of them at once, nor ask many similar questions, or the chorus of ghostly laughter will be overwhelming. I imagine the answer would be something like Hamlet's: 'You yourselves, sir, shall be as wise as we were, if, like crabs, you could go backward.' It is thought something wonderful that uneducated persons should believe in witchcraft in the nineteenth century: as if educated persons did not believe in grosser follies: such as this same spirit-rapping, unknown tongues, clairvoyance, table-turning, and all sorts of fanatical impositions, having for the present their climax in Mormonism. Herein all times are alike. There is nothing too monstrous for human credulity. I like the notion of the Aristophanic comedy. But it would require a numerous company, especially as the chorus is indispensable. The *tenson* may be carried on by two.

MR. GRYLL

I do not see why we should not have both.

MISS GRYLL

Oh pray, Doctor! let us have the comedy. We hope to have a houseful at Christmas, and I think we may get it up well, chorus and all. I should so like to hear what my great ancestor, Gryllus, thinks of us: and Homer, and Dante, and Shakespeare, and Richard the First, and Oliver Cromwell.

THE REVEREND DOCTOR OPIMIAN

A very good *dramatis personæ*. With these, and the help of one or two Athenians and Romans, we may arrive at a tolerable judgment on our own immeasurable superiority to everything that has gone before us.

Before we proceed further, we will give some account of our interlocutors.

*Gryll Grange*, ch. I

Peacock's mottoes are often appropriate for the chapters they precede, but many times they seem appended simply because Peacock wanted to append them. He might have said with the narrator of Byron's *Don Juan*, 'I love to quote,' for he quotes continually—and from half a dozen languages. The passage from Petronius that heads 'Misnomers' is hardly relevant to the discussion at the Gryll's dinner table, at least no one seems to worry about gathering rosebuds, but it does have an oblique importance to the chapter.

Doctor Opimian owes his name, appropriately, to a Roman wine, a wine famous for its quality, which the Roman *parvenu* serves his guests in *The Satyricon*. Peacock certainly seems to have Petronius in mind when he presents this dinner conversation between Gryll and the worldly cleric. In one important way, however, *Gryll Grange* is farther from *The Satyricon* than Peacock's earlier conversational novels. Though Opimian is, to use his own words against him, capable of 'furious political dogmatism', and though he is similarly a confirmed pedant, he is presented with less irony than Peacock's cranks usually are. We see this more clearly as the novel progresses, but one clue is already present: both Squire Gryll and Morgana Gryll

(Peacock's heroines usually sport such absurd names) concur with the Doctor's theories, disagreeing only in details. In the earlier books the dialectic might have been less formal—less of a well-mannered exchange—it would have been more of an intellectual brawl. Escot and Foster never could agree, never do at least within the course of *Headlong Hall*. Gryll and Opimian argue, assuming basic accord. It is, as Miss Gryll observes, a matter of musical variations upon a basic theme.

*Gryll Grange* begins with conversation and proceeds by conversation to such an extent that the narrator introduces his 'interlocutors' only after an entire chapter has gone by. As though sitting in the wings, the narrator lets the spotlight shine on the characters, whose voices supplant his own. The corollary of this is of course that the speakers tend to become a composite of the narrator. Less true of *Headlong Hall*, in which the narrator chuckles in a constant aside, it is almost wholly true of *Gryll Grange*. In his final novel Peacock exploits the earlier method but is far more tolerant of his characters and their viewpoints.

The 'Aristophanic Comedy', proposed by Squire Gryll and actually performed later in the story, becomes an extension of what Opimian and the Grylls call a *tenson*: that is, an impromptu debate in verse on a given subject. Most of the chapters are themselves *tensons*, and the first certainly is, although it would be difficult to name a winner. What is true in *Gryll Grange*, in this respect, is true of the early stories, as well. Peacock always delighted in verbal games. In *Maid Marian*, for example, Friar Tuck responds to one of the baron's puns with this outburst:

'Punnest thou?' said the friar. 'A heinous anti-christian offence. Why anti-christian? Because anti-catholic. Why anti-catholic? Because anti-roman. Why anti-roman? Because Carthaginian. Is no pun from Punic? *punica fides*:

the very quint-essential quiddity of bad faith: double-visaged: double-tongued. He that will make a pun will——I say no more. Fie on it.'

Peacock and his characters pun, sometimes quietly, sometimes—as Friar Tuck illustrates—with a prodigious mouthful; and since his people are in constant competition and always interrupting one another, Peacock insists on the aspect of play. There are more than verbal games in his novels. He has archery contests, chess, dances, bardic conferences, and wrestling matches. And he uses them, as he uses the conversational exchanges, to effect a final happy ending and a general reconciliation. Games, accordingly, become a part of the total ritual, and the ritual is that of comedy.

# *Peacock's satire*

Satire may be approached in several different ways. Usually it is associated with criticism (burlesque, invective, etc.), or with literary genres (either verse, or formal satire, or Menippean satire, which we have termed a catch-all for prose and fictional genres of various sorts). Peacock wrote several types of satire. His poems *Sir Proteus* and the *Paper-Money Lyrics* approximate formal satire, as in a different way do some of his essays, including 'The Four Ages of Poetry'. But we are concerned here mainly with the fiction, and Peacock's fiction is closely related to Menippean satire—with some important differences.

When we speak about Peacock's satire we are tempted to identify satiric targets, or specific satiric techniques, to identify Scythrop as Shelley and Mr. Toogood as Robert Owen. This is a necessary part of criticism. If satire works well, however, and if it lasts, as Peacock's has, it does so as successful literature. Just as no one would appreciate *David Copperfield* because Uriah Heap might represent a typical Victorian hypocrite, so no one would read *Nightmare Abbey* because, or only because, Scythrop offers a telling caricature of Shelley. *Nightmare Abbey* does not of course work in the same way that *David Copperfield* works, but unless we understand how the whole book is put together, unless we understand the relationship of parts, we shall involve ourselves in serious misreading.

Satire has been a recurrent topic in earlier sections, in part because it underlines or is intimately connected with other features of Peacock's narrative. The way he writes satire is linked to the way he creates his novelistic world, to his way of telling a story, and to his insistence upon a comic resolution. In other words, what has already been said about satire in the earlier sections has been based on the assumption that satiric fiction is something more than a random collection of critical statements, that it has, like any art form, its own conventions, and that it involves the entire means of presenting a story.

In his study of satire, *The Cankered Muse*, Professor Alvin Kernan suggests three categories useful for the identifying and criticising of satire. He speaks of the satiric scene, the satirist (or ironic narrator), and the satiric plot. We have shown to what extent his narrator can be considered a conventional satiric narrator, and have argued that Peacock's plot and scene differ from those of conventional satiric fiction. But it will help to put these observations in a more specific context.

Satire traditionally comes to no conclusion. Things remain the same, or, in satire's own way, they become even more the same—a little worse than at the beginning. Doctor Johnson is being exemplary when he ends *Rasselas* with 'A Conclusion in which Nothing is Concluded'. Neither in *Rasselas* nor in *Gulliver's Travels* nor in *Gargantua* do we see any resolution. Satire often approaches romance and comedy; often it approaches tragedy. But it differs in at least one respect by offering no conclusions, no earth-shaking deaths, no fulfilled quests, no laughing weddings. When, after the following sequence in *Melincourt*, the enfranchised mob has been appeased by ale and sent off on its business, Peacock's group can go unconcernedly on its way. But unlike, say, Johnson's group in *Rasselas*, Peacock's is coming closer to worldly 'happiness'. Peacock may introduce them into awful circumstances, but he looks after them carefully. Anthelia Melincourt, heroine of this book, manages to get abducted, and she comes perilously close to losing her virtue. But no. Rescue in the nick of time—celebrations—weddings—happily-ever-after. When we consider what Voltaire (whom Peacock admired) did with his wretched people, Peacock's seem lightly-handled indeed. Whatever has been aggravated, whatever has bared its bottom for a whipping, is, by the conclusion, settled once again. In short, Peacock's satire never insists upon its assumptions, never concludes upon the logic of its criticism. His books are satires in only a limited sense.

It is with his satiric scene as it is with plot. Peacock hovers in the area of satire but maintains a distance. Whereas satirists like Petronius and Rabelais offer an intentionally confused and bewildering array of details in their presentation of scene, Peacock, prefers fewer details and more general classifications. The difference here, however, lies in degree rather than kind. Peacock's scene always includes some disarray, some fantastic assortment of sights and sounds. His satire, though presented differently, and much more briefly, depends like Rabelais' on an established confusion. 'Onevote' illustrates this very well.

*Melincourt* was Peacock's second completed novel. Both before and after working on *Headlong Hall*, he had attempted a story entitled 'Satyrane' or 'Calidore', the theme of which involved an innocent coming in contact with 'civilisation'. *Melincourt* also has its innocent, Sir Oran Haut-ton, bart, who is, as his name implies, a benobled orang-outang. Sir Oran offers a burlesque of the notions, not only of Buffon and Rousseau, but also of Lord Monboddo, a Rousseauistic semi-anthropologist—and a Scot—whose *Origins of Language* Peacock quotes, in mock-scholarly footnotes, throughout. Sir Oran's literary forbears include Spenser's Satyrane (the wild gentleman in Book One of the *Fairie Queene*) and, perhaps more pertinently, Voltaire's American innocent, L'Ingenu, and Robert Bage's hero—also an American innocent—in *Hermsprong*.

Peacock is caricaturing his literary models as much as he caricatures the philosophical theorists; however much he makes Sir Oran into a sympathetic (if silent) character, he also keeps him a figure of low burlesque—that is, an ape. In the following passage from *Melincourt*, Sir Oran has travelled with his friends to the Borough of Onevote, in order to be elected to Parliament. Predictably, his natural instincts get the better of civilised restraint.

## 8

### *'The Borough of Onevote'*

The heath had very much the appearance of a race ground;[1] with booths and stalls, the voices of pie-men and apple-women, the grinding of barrel organs, the scraping of fiddles, the squeaking of ballad-singers, the chirping of corkscrews, the vociferations of ale-drinkers, the cries of the 'last dying speeches of desperate malefactors', and of 'The History and Antiquities of the honourable Borough of Onevote,[2] a full and circumstantial account, all in half a sheet, for the price of one halfpenny!'

The hustings were erected in proper form, and immedi-

[1] This is not the beginning of the chapter.

[2] That is, a pocket borough.

ately opposite to them was an enormous marquee with a small opening in front, in which was seated the important person of Mr. Christopher Corporate, with a tankard of ale and a pipe. The ladies remained in the barouche under the care of Sir Telegraph and Mr. Hippy. Mr. Forester, Mr. Fax, and Sir Oran Haut-ton, joined Mr. Sarcastic on the hustings.

Mr. Sarcastic stepped forward amidst the shouts of the assembled crowd, and addressed Mr. Christopher Corporate:

'Free, fat, and dependent burgess of this ancient and honourable borough! I stand forward an unworthy candidate, to be the representative of so important a personage, who comprises in himself a three hundredth part of the whole elective capacity of this extensive empire. For if the whole population be estimated at eleven millions, with what awe and veneration must I look on one, who is, as it were, the abstract and quintessence of thirty-three thousand six hundred and sixty-six people! The voice of Stentor was like the voice of fifty, and the voice of Harry Gill[3] was like the voice of three; but what are these to the voice of Mr. Christopher Corporate, which gives utterance in one breath to the concentrated power of thirty-three thousand six hundred and sixty-six voices? Of such an one it may indeed be said, that *he is himself an host*, and that *none but himself can be his parallel.*

'Most potent, grave, and reverend signor! it is usual on these occasions to make a great vapouring about honour and conscience: but as those words are now generally acknowledged to be utterly destitute of meaning, I have too much respect for your understanding to say any thing about them. The *monied interest*, Mr. Corporate, for which you are as illustrious *as the sun at noon-day*, is the great point of connexion and sympathy between us: and no circumstances can throw a *wet blanket* on the ardour of our reciprocal esteem, while the *fundamental feature* of our

[3] See Mr. Wordsworth's *Lyrical Ballads.* [Peacock.]

mutual interests presents itself to us in so *tangible a shape*.[4] How high a value I set upon your voice, you may judge by the price I have paid for half of it: which, indeed, deeply lodged as my feelings are in my pocket, I yet see no reason to regret, since you will thus confer on mine, a transmutable and marketable value, which I trust with proper management will leave me no loser by the bargain.'

'Huzza!' said Mr. Corporate.

'People of the city of Novote!' proceeded Mr. Sarcastic, 'some of you, I am informed, consider yourselves aggrieved, that, while your large and populous city has no share whatever in the formation of the Honourable House, the *plural unity* of Mr. Christopher Corporate should be invested with the privilege of double representation. But, gentlemen, representation is of two kinds, actual, and virtual: an important distinction, and of great political consequence.

'The Honourable Baronet and myself being the actual representatives of the fat burgess of Onevote, shall be the virtual representatives of the worthy citizens of Novote; and you may rely on it, gentlemen, (*with his hand on his heart*,) we shall always be deeply attentive to your interests, when they happen, as no doubt they sometimes will, to be perfectly compatible with our own.

'A member of Parliament, gentlemen, to speak to you in your own phrase, is a sort of staple commodity, manufactured for home consumption. Much has been said of the improvement of machinery in the present age, by which one man may do the work of a dozen. If this be admirable, and admirable it is acknowledged to be by all the civilised world, how much more admirable is the improvement of political machinery, by which one man does the work of thirty thousand! I am sure, I need not say another word to a great manufacturing population like the inhabitants of the city of Novote, to convince them of the beauty and utility of this most luminous arrangement.

[4] The figures of speech marked in Italics are familiar to the admirers of parliamentary rhetoric. [Peacock.]

'The duty of a representative of the people, whether actual or virtual, is simply *to tax*. Now this important branch of public business is much more easily and expeditiously transacted by the means of virtual, than it possibly could be by that of actual representation. For when the minister draws up his scheme of ways and means, he will do it with much more celerity and confidence, when he knows that the propitious countenance of virtual representation will never cease to smile upon him as long as he continues in place, than if he had to encounter the doubtful aspect of actual representation, which might, perhaps, look black on some of his favourite projects, thereby greatly impeding the distribution of secret service money at home, and placing foreign legitimacy in a very awkward predicament. The carriage of the state would then be like a chariot in a forest, turning to the left for a troublesome thorn, and to the right for a sturdy oak; whereas it now rolls forward like the car of Juggernaut over the plain, crushing whatever offers to impede its way.

'The constitution says that no man shall be taxed but by his own consent: a very plausible theory, gentlemen, but not reducible to practice. Who will apply a lancet to his own arm, and bleed himself? Very few, you acknowledge. Who then, *à fortiori*, would apply a lancet to his own pocket, and draw off what is dearer to him than his blood—his money? Fewer still of course: I humbly opine, none. —What then remains but to appoint a royal college of state surgeons, who may operate on the patient according to their views of his case? Taxation is political phlebotomy: the Honourable House is, figuratively speaking, a royal college of state surgeons. A good surgeon must have firm nerves and a steady hand; and, perhaps, the less feeling the better. Now, it is manifest, that, as all feeling is founded on sympathy, the fewer constituents a representative has, the less must be his sympathy with the public, and the less, of course, as is desirable, his feeling for his patient—the people:—who, therefore, with so much *sangfroid*, can phlebotomize the nation, as the representative of half an elector?

'Gentlemen, as long as a *full Gazette* is pleasant to the *quidnunc;* as long as an empty purse is delightful to the spendthrift; as long as the cry of *Question* is a satisfactory *answer* to an argument, and to outvote reason, is to refute it; as long as the way to pay old debts is to incur new ones of five times the amount; as long as the grand recipes of political health and longevity are *bleeding* and *hot water* —so long must you rejoice in the privileges of Mr. Christopher Corporate, so long must you acknowledge, from the very bottom of your pockets, the benefits and blessings of *virtual representation*.'

This harangue was received with great applause, acclamations rent the air, and ale flowed in torrents. Mr. Forester declined speaking, and the party on the hustings proceeded to business. Sir Oran Haut-ton, Baronet, and Simon Sarcastic, Esquire, were nominated in form. Mr. Christopher Corporate held up both his hands, with his tankard in one, and his pipe in the other: and neither poll nor scrutiny being demanded, the two candidates were pronounced duly elected, as representatives of the ancient and honourable borough of Onevote.

The shouts were renewed: the ale flowed rapidly: the pipe and tankard of Mr. Corporate were replenished. Sir Oran Haut-ton, Baronet, M.P. bowed gracefully to the people with his hand on his heart.

A cry was now raised of 'Chair 'em! chair 'em!' when Mr. Sarcastic again stepped forward.

'Gentlemen!' said he, 'a slight difficulty opposes itself to the honour you would confer on us. The members should, according to form, be chaired by their electors: and how can one elector, great man as he is, chair two representatives? But to obviate this dilemma as well as circumstances admit, I move that the "large body corporate of one" whom the Honourable Baronet and myself have the honour to represent, do resolve himself into a committee.'

He had no sooner spoken, than the marquee opened, and a number of bulky personages, all in dress, aspect, size, and figure, very exact resemblances of Mr. Christopher Corporate, each with his pipe and his tankard, emerged into daylight, who encircling their venerable prototype, lifted their tankards high in air, and pronounced with Stentorian symphony, 'HAIL, PLURAL UNIT!' Then, after a simultaneous draught, throwing away their pipes and tankards, for which the mob immediately scrambled, they raised on high two magnificent chairs, and prepared to carry into effect the last ceremony of the election. The party on the hustings descended. Mr. Sarcastic stepped into his chair; and his part of the procession, headed by Mr. Christopher Corporate, and surrounded by a multiform and many-coloured crowd, moved slowly off towards the city of Novote, amidst the undistinguishable clamour of multitudinous voices.

Sir Oran Haut-ton watched the progress of his precursor, as his chair rolled and swayed over the sea of heads, like a boat with one mast on a stormy ocean; and the more he watched the agitation of its movements, the more his countenance gave indications of strong dislike to the process: so that when his seat in the second chair was offered to him, he with a very polite bow declined the honour. The party that was to carry him, thinking that his repugnance arose entirely from diffidence, proceeded with gentle force to overcome his scruples, when not precisely penetrating their motives, and indignant at this attempt to violate the freedom of the natural man, he seized a stick from a sturdy farmer at his elbow, and began to lay about him with great vigour and effect. Those who escaped being knocked down by the first sweep of his weapon, ran away with all their might, but were soon checked by the pressure of the crowd, who, hearing the noise of conflict, and impatient to ascertain the cause, bore down from all points upon a common centre, and formed a circumferential pressure that effectually prohibited the egress of those within; and they in their turn, in their eagerness to escape from Sir Oran (who, like Artegall's Iron Man, or like Ajax among the Trojans, or like Rhodomont in Paris, or like Orlando among the soldiers of Agramant, kept clearing for himself an ample space, in the midst of the encircling crowd), waged desperate conflict with those without;[5] so that from the equal and opposite action of the centripetal and centrifugal forces, resulted a stationary combat, raging between the circumferences of two concentric circles, with barbaric dissonance of deadly feud, and infinite variety of oath and execration, till Sir Oran, charging desperately along one of the radii, fought a free passage through all opposition; and rushing to the barouche of Sir Telegraph Paxarett, sprang to his old station on the box, from whence he shook his sapling at the foe, with looks of mortal defiance. Mr. Forester, who had been forcibly parted from him at the commencement of the strife, and had been all anxiety on his account, mounted with great alacrity to his station on the roof: the rest of the party was already seated: the Honourable Mrs. Pinmoney, half-fainting with terror, earnestly entreated Sir Telegraph to fly: Sir Telegraph cracked his whip: the horses sprang forward like racers: the wheels went round like the wheels of a firework. The tumult of battle lessening as they receded, came wafted to them on the wings of the wind: for the flame of discord having been once kindled, was not extinguished by the departure of its first flambeau—Sir Oran; but war raged wide and far, here in the thickest mass of central fight, there in the light skirmishing of flying detachments. The hustings were demolished, and the beams and planks turned into offensive weapons: the booths were torn to pieces, and the canvass converted into flags floating over the heads of magnanimous heroes that rushed to revenge they knew not what, in deadly battle with they knew not whom. The stalls and barrows were upset; and

[5] Peacock's references are to Spenser's *Fairie Queene*, to the *Iliad*, and to Ariosto's *Orlando Furioso*. He has several such 'mock epic' passages.

the pears, apples, oranges, mutton-pies, and masses of gingerbread, flew like missiles of fate in all directions. The *sanctum sanctorum* of the ale was broken into, and the guardians of the Hesperian liquor were put to ignominious rout. Hats and wigs were hurled into the air, never to return to the heads from which they had suffered violent divorce. The collision of sticks, the ringing of empty ale-casks, the shrieks of women, and the vociferations of combatants, mingled in one deepening and indescribable tumult: till at length, every thing else being levelled with the heath, they turned the mingled torrent of their wrath on the cottage of Mr. Corporate, to which they triumphantly set fire, and danced round the blaze, like a rabble of village boys round the effigy of the immortal Guy. In a few minutes the ancient and honourable borough of Onevote was reduced to ashes: but we have the satisfaction to state that it was rebuilt a few days afterwards, at the joint expense of its two representatives, and His Grace the Duke of Rottenburgh.

*Melincourt*, ch. XXII

Dickens, when he wrote about the rambling adventures of the Pickwick Club, may have had the format of several earlier writers in mind—Cobbett, with his rural rides, perhaps among them. He may also have been familiar with Peacock, for there are scenes, especially in *Melincourt*, close to the antic scenes in *Pickwick*. Compare, for example, Peacock's description of 'Onevote' with the 'Eatanswill' episode.

Dickens's is, as always, a much more complex or detailed scene. His narrator introduces Pickwick and Pickwick's disciples into the electioneering, then as it were, opens the floodgates of impressions. Peacock maintains a clearer and smaller focus, only sketching the details. He is to Dickens as George Cruikshank is to Hogarth. Peacock's narrator is, however, as amused as Dickens's; beholding the confusion and ridiculing the mob, as he belittles the system catering to the mob. Both offer absurd speeches (though in the confusion, Dickens keeps his unheard), tussles, and political fopperies. Peacock might have laughed at precisely the same idiocies as Dickens had *Melincourt* been written after the 1832 Reform Bill. Both writers, too, change their means of narrative somewhere towards the middle of the scene, abandoning the specifically satiric for the farcically humorous. When, for example, Sir Oran is about to be chaired, Peacock's narrative shifts to the mock-heroic, and as it seems to become more logical, it becomes increasingly more absurd. Sir Oran's action *is* logical in its way, but that is not in the same way as Mr. Sarcastic's clearheaded denunciation of a whole political system. Whereas Dickens lets his scene become a bewildering confusion, Peacock puts blinders on his narrator. He describes Sir Oran as something resembling an epic hero, fighting the good fight. We never forget of course that Sir Oran is an orang-outang, and the result is a grotesque discrepancy between the account and its object. Dickens seems to give himself up to the humour, while Peacock keeps at least one eye on a satiric target.

Peacock's targets in *Melincourt* differ somewhat from his usual targets, at least in emphasis. Peacock generally excludes comment about specific political inequities or merely comments in passing; and therefore the particular framework of the 'Onevote' incident is peculiar to *Melincourt* (except as it ends in physical upheaval). But many things here recur throughout his stories. He always laughs at false rhetoric—delighting in it at the same time; he usually drags in Wordsworth and Coleridge for at least a short drubbing; he parodies current ideas, philosophical or literary, along with new fashions and fads; and like most satirists, he finds some way of ridiculing the idea of progress—and certainly the idea that progress is the automatic concomitant of time.

Laughter at the expense of false optimism is important to Peacock's work, and it helps to relate pieces as disparate as 'The Four Ages of Poetry' and *Gryll Grange*. Peacock was never a theoretician, never a systematic thinker. He changed his attack, and even the grounds for his attack, as he responded to innovations and change. And in a sense, intellectual as he was, it is really an attitude that underlies his response, a skepticism and a doubt. He was sanguine about none of the early nineteenth-century props, be it Christianity, politics, or industry. Consider, for example, the implications of the 'Onevote' episode. Peacock quite obviously ridicules the mob. Yet his political outlook in this sequence (and throughout *Melincourt*) is that of a political radical. He is at once bemoaning a corrupt political system and wanting a change in that system which would give power to those he finds incapable of its proper use. This, or this sort of, dilemma underlies all his writing. In *Gryll Grange*, almost fifty years later, he has as little good to say about the 'reformed' establishment as he had had in *Melincourt* about the unreformed. Certainly he has little hope of future improvement. He is much closer in *Gryll Grange* to the Tory line, but really he is no Tory, just as he was no true radical. Group thinking and group faith remained anathaema to him.

Peacock was, and he needs to be understood as, a commentator on his times, training the guns of laughter on whatever seemed most absurd at the time of writing. Yet, both uncommitted and nostalgic, he tempers his criticism as he alters the structure of his satire, and the resulting wry wit and amused tolerance combine to explain the otherwise inscrutable writer.

# *Chronological outline of Peacock's life*

1785 Born October 18, at Weymouth in Dorsetshire.

1788 After the death of his father, a glass merchant, removed with his mother to Chertsey, a village on the Thames some twenty miles from London. Spent most of his life in this area.

1791–96 Attended school, his first and last, at Englefield Green. The headmaster, John Wicks, said 'he would prove one of the most remarkable men of his day'.

1800 Employed briefly as a clerk in London. Won a prize for a poem, 'Is History or Biography the more Improving Study?' published in *The Juvenile Library*.

1800–05? Lived in London.

1804 Published *The Monks of St. Mark*, a humorous poem anticipating the farce in his novels.

1805 *Palmyra and other Poems* published. Returned to Chertsey.

1806 Took a summer walking tour of Scotland.

1807 Began friendship with Edward and Thomas Hookham, who were to publish some of his writings. Love affair with Fanny Falkner, later recorded in the poem 'Newark Abbey'.

1808–9 Secretary aboard the H.M.S. *Venerable*, a warship anchored off the Downs, which he called a 'floating Inferno'. Wrote dramatic prologues and humorous poems.

1809 Excursion along the Thames for poetic material. Afterwards visited Wales for several months and met his future wife.

1810 *The Genius of the Thames* published.

1811–13 Worked on two farces, later incorporated into *Headlong Hall*.

1812 *The Philosophy of Melancholy* published. Met Shelley for the first time in London.

1813 Another visit to Wales. *Sir Hornbook* published, a humorous 'grammatico-allegorical ballad' for children. Travelled with Shelley and some of his friends to the Lake District and Scotland.

1814 *Sir Proteus* published, a satiric attack on Southey, anticipatory of Byron's *Vision of Judgment*. Contemplated founding a school in the Lakes. Strain in friendship with Shelley when Shelley eloped with Mary Godwin.

1815 Arrested for debt after an affair with an unknown woman. Probably began at about this time to accept a stipend from Shelley. Removed to the village of Marlow, within walking distance of Shelley's house at Bishopgate. Thomas Jefferson Hogg, mutual friend of Shelley and Peacock, called their winter of 1815–16 'a mere Atticism'.

1816 *Headlong Hall* published. Also *The Round Table*, a comic account of the kings of England for children. Worked on *Melincourt*. Harriet Shelley died. Shelley married Mary Godwin, who never liked Peacock.

1817 *Melincourt* published, 'by the author of *Headlong Hall*'. Shelley's *Laon and Cythna*, Peacock's *Rhodo-*

*daphne: or the Thessalian Spirit* written during the summer and fall at a time of close cooperation.

1818 *Rhododaphne* published; said by one reviewer to put to shame 'our Scotts, Southeys, Byrons, Moores, Campbells, Wordsworths'. *Nightmare Abbey* published. Shelleys left once again for Italy. Wrote a diary for the summer and began his first essay 'On Fashionable Literature', which he never finished. Worked on the first half of *Maid Marian*. Began his thirty-seven year employment with the East India Company.

1820 Married Jane Gryffyd after a seven year separation. 'The Four Ages of Poetry' published in *Olliers' Miscellany*.

1821 Took another trip to Wales. Resumed work on *Maid Marian*.

1822 *Maid Marian* published, then adapted for the theatre. Birth of his first child. Purchased house in Lower Halliford. Shelley died in February. Peacock, with Byron, executor of the estate. Busied himself on behalf of Mary Shelley and won her grudging respect.

1825–26 Worked on *Paper-Money Lyrics*, a collection of satiric poems not published until 1837.

1826 Death of his daughter Margaret.

1827 Scathing review of Thomas Moore's *The Epicurean*, to be followed in 1830 by a similar attack on Moore's *Byron*.

1829–36 Wrote music criticism, mainly of the opera, first for *The Globe*, later for *The Examiner*.

1829 *The Misfortunes of Elphin* published.

1830 Essays in *The Westminster Review* on Moore, Thomas Jefferson, and London Bridge.

1831 *Crotchet Castle* published.

1833 Death of his mother.

1835 A technical essay on Steam Navigation published in

the *Edinburgh Review*. An essay on 'French Comic Romances' published in *The London Review*.

1836 Succeeded James Mill as Examiner, a high post in the India House (was himself later succeeded by John Stuart Mill). 'The Epicier' published in *The London Review*. Wrote the autobiographical essay, 'The Abbey House: Recollections of Childhood'.

1837 *Paper-Money Lyrics* published.

1838–50 Published nothing for twelve years.

1839 Met and established a friendship with John Cam Hobhouse, Lord Broughton, a former friend of Byron.

1849 Marriage of his daughter Mary to George Meredith —an unhappy match.

1851 'Gastronomy and Civilization' published. Worked on a cookbook that he never completed.

1852 Began a series of essays on the drama for *Fraser's Magazine* called *Horae Dramaticae*; finished one on Roman, two on Greek plays.

1856 Retired from the India House.

1858 Wrote the first part of the Shelley Memoirs, a corrective essay 'to protest against this system of biographical gossip'. Published several literary reviews.

1861 *Gryll Grange* published, after appearing serially in *Fraser's* the preceding year. Began several narratives in these years. Wrote another autobiographical essay, 'The Last Day of Windsor Forest'.

1862 *Gl'Ingannati*, or *The Deceived*, published: a prose translation of the Italian play.

1866 Died January 23 at Lower Halliford.

# Bibliography

## A *Editions*

* *The Works of Thomas Love Peacock*, edited and with an introduction and notes by H. F. B. Brett-Smith and C. E. Jones (the Halliford Edition, 1924–34), is the standard edition. It superseded earlier and less complete editions by Henry Cole (1875) and Richard Garnett (1891). The Halliford Edition contains all the novels, all the known poems and fragments (with some small exceptions), and most of the letters, essays, and miscellaneous prose. A fine piece of work, it is unfortunately both hard to find and, when found, expensive.

* *The Novels of Thomas Love Peacock*, edited and with introductions and notes by David Garnett, London, Rupert Hart-Davis (Harvest Books, 1963) is the best available edition of Peacock's novels. It has better and generally more complete notes than the Halliford Edition, and Garnett's introductions are excellent. There are other inexpensive editions of the novels published in England and the United States, but none of comparable quality.

* denotes works of first importance.

*Peacock's 'Four Ages of Poetry', Shelley's 'Defence of Poetry', and Browning's 'Essay on Shelley'*, ed. intro. H. F. B. Brett-Smith, Oxford, Blackwells (1953), and *'A Defence of Poetry'* . . . and *'The Four Ages of Poetry'*, ed., intro. John E. Jordan, New York, Library of Liberal Arts (1965) both offer inexpensive reprints of Peacock's essay. His other essays are available only in the Halliford Edition.

B *Memoirs and biographical studies*

BUCHANAN, ROBERT, 'Thomas Love Peacock: a Personal Reminiscence', *A Look Round Literature*, London, Ward and Downey (1887), pp. 162–184. One of few accounts by contemporaries.

NICHOLS, ELEANOR, contributing editor, *Shelley and His Circle 1773–1822*, 2 vols, edited by Kenneth N. Cameron, Cambridge, Harvard University Press (1961). Includes a valuable biographical and critical essay.

PECK, WALTER E., 'A Note on Shelley and Peacock', *Modern Language Notes*, XXXVI (June, 1921), 371–73. A brief but helpful note about their collaboration.

STRACHEY, SIR EDWARD, 'Recollections of Thomas Love Peacock', introduction to *Calidore and Miscellanea*, ed. R. Garnett, London, Dent (1891).

* VAN DOREN, CARL, *The Life of Thomas Love Peacock*, London, J. M. Dent; New York, E. P. Dutton (1965). As much a critical study as a biography, this remains the standard life. It is corrected by the long biographical introduction to the Halliford Edition.

WRIGHT, HERBERT, 'The Associations of Thomas Love Peacock with Wales', *Essays and Studies by Members of the English Association*, Oxford, Clarendon Press (1926), vol. XII, pp. 24–26. An excellent account of Peacock's visits, studies, and attitudes toward Wales, including a discussion of *The Misfortunes of Elphin*.

## C *Critical studies*

### 1 *Full-length studies*

CAMPBELL, OLWEN W., *Thomas Love Peacock*, London, Arthur Baker; New York, Roy Publishers (1953). A short introduction.

FREEMAN, A. MARTIN, *Thomas Love Peacock, a Critical Study*, London, Martin Secker; New York, Mitchell Kennerly (1911). An appreciative and balanced account; one of the earliest full-length studies and still one of the best.

MAYOUX, JEAN-JACQUES, *Un Epicurien anglais: Thomas Love Peacock*, Paris, Nizet et Bastard (1933). An exhaustive history of Peacock's reading, writing, and thinking, especially good on 'sources'. A typically French thesis, and available only in French.

* PRIESTLEY, J. B., *Thomas Love Peacock*, London, Macmillans (1927), English Men of Letters Series. Includes some of the best discussions of Peacock's novels, though not uniformly reliable.

READ, BILL, *The Critical Reputation of Thomas Love Peacock with an Annotated Enumerative Bibliography*, unpublished doctoral dissertation at Boston University (1959). An extremely useful work. Read has issued 'Thomas Love Peacock: an Enumerative Bibliography' in the *Bulletin of Bibliography*; Part II, 'Works about Thomas Love Peacock', appears in XXIV (1964), 70–91.

### 2 *Essays and book chapters*

AMIS, KINGSLEY, 'Laugh When You Can', *Spectator*, CXCIV (April 1, 1955), 402–404. Peacock is 'somebody far more energetically original than the chorus of drowsy Victorian and Edwardian eulogy would imply'. A brief and witty call for better criticism.

BELL, CLIVE, 'Peacock', *Pot-Boilers*, London, Chatto and Windus (1918).

DYSON, A. E., 'Peacock', *The Crazy Fabric, Essays in Irony*, London (1965). Though he takes his title from Peacock, Dyson is mostly negative in his discussion. An important criticism.

HOUSE, HUMPHREY, 'The Works of Peacock', *Listener*, XLII (December 8, 1949), 997–98. A clear and sometimes unflattering assessment. He suggests that Hazlitt offers the best introduction to Peacock.

JACK, IAN, 'PEACOCK', *English Literature, 1815–1832*, Oxford, the Clarendon Press (1963). One of the best critical essays on Peacock and an important re-assessment of his position in early nineteenth-century literature.

NEWBOLT, SIR HENRY, 'Peacock, Scott, and Robin Hood', *Studies in Green and Grey*, London, Thomas Nelson (1926). An appreciative account of Peacock's relation to Scott, with specific reference to *Maid Marian* and *Ivanhoe*.

PRIESTLEY, J. B., 'Seithenyn', *English Comic Characters*, London, John Lane (1925). An exuberant discussion of Seithenyn, Falstaff, and other great topers.

RALEIGH, SIR WALTER, 'Lecture Notes on Thomas Love Peacock', *On Writing and Writers*, London, Edward Arnold (1926). Speaks of Peacock's 'spirit of mischief'; though he mocks idealists and makers of systems, he has 'a great love for ideas'.

SAINTSBURY, GEORGE, 'Thomas Love Peacock', *Collected Essays and Papers*, London, Toronto, and New York, J. M. Dent (1923), vol. II. Saintsbury also edited and wrote introductions for Peacock's novels. His discussions are useful, original—and dated.

STEWART, J. I. M., *Thomas Love Peacock*, London, Longmans, Green (1963), Writers and their Work Series. A brief pamphlet.

WILSON, EDMUND, 'The Musical Glasses of Thomas Love Peacock', *Classics and Commercials*, New York, Anchor Books (1951). Relates Peacock's love of music, especially Mozart's, to the design of his novels. Praises the heroines, which he calls perhaps the most attractive in nineteenth-century fiction.

## D *Works with important mention of Peacock*

ABLE, AUGUSTUS H., *George Meredith and Thomas Love Peacock: a Study in Literary Influence*, Philadelphia, University of Pennsylvania (1933). Dull, but useful for reference.

ABRAMS, MEYER H., *The Mirror and the Lamp: Romantic Theory and the Critical Tradition*, New York, Oxford, (1953). Includes a discussion of Peacock's irony in 'The Four Ages', with reference to Shelley's 'Defence'.

BAKER, ERNEST A., *The History of the English Novel*, New York (1937; rev. ed. 1950); one of the most reliable appraisals by a literary historian.

BUSH, DOUGLAS, *Mythology and the Romantic Tradition in English Poetry*, Cambridge, Harvard Press (1937). Includes an informative account of *Rhododaphne*.

FRYE, NORTHROP, *The Anatomy of Criticism*, Princeton (1957). Two chapters are relevant: 'The Mythos of Winter', a discussion of satire and irony, and 'The Four Forms of Prose Fiction', which argues Peacock's relationship to Rabelais and other writers of Menippean satire.

KERNAN, ALVIN, *The Cankered Muse, Satire of the English Renaissance*, New Haven, Yale (1959). Mentions Peacock only incidentally, but offers an invaluable introduction to satire.

KITCHEN, GEORGE, *Burlesque and Parody in English,* London (1931). A useful historical guide, with several short discussions of Peacock.

NOTOPOLOUS, JAMES A., *The Platonism of Shelley: a Study of Platonism and the Poetic Mind,* Durham, N. C. (1940). Offers a helpful account of the literary relationship between Shelley and Peacock, including a slightly exaggerated description of Peacock's 'platonism'.

PRAZ, MARIO, *The Hero in Eclipse in Victorian Fiction,* trans. Angus Davidson, London (1956). A misguided but provocative attack.

SICKELS, ELEANOR M., *The Gloomy Egoist: Moods and Themes of Melancholy from Gray to Keats.* Discusses Peacock's early poems as the culmination of several eighteenth-century poetic traditions.

SUTHERLAND, JAMES, *English Satire,* Cambridge (1962). Helpful, but not at his best on Peacock.

WHITE, NEWMAN IVEY, *Shelley,* New York, Alfred Knopf (1940). Includes relevant biographical information.